The Way Forward:

Embracing Unity, Faith, and Power

O'Niel Fisher

iUniverse, Inc.
Bloomington

iUniverse books may be ordered through booksellers or by contacting:

iUniverse
1663 Liberty Drive
Bloomington, IN 47403
www.iuniverse.com
1-800-Authors (1-800-288-4677)

Because of the dynamic nature of the Internet, any web addresses or links contained in this book may have changed since publication and may no longer be valid. The views expressed in this work are solely those of the author and do not necessarily reflect the views of the publisher, and the publisher hereby disclaims any responsibility for them.

Any people depicted in stock imagery provided by Thinkstock are models, and such images are being used for illustrative purposes only. Certain stock imagery © Thinkstock.

Cover designed by Kevin Mahoney Nunes

ISBN: 978-1-4620-7173-9 (sc)
ISBN: 978-1-4620-7175-3 (hc)
ISBN: 978-1-4620-7174-6 (ebook)

Library of Congress Control Number: 2011961813

Printed in the United States of America

iUniverse rev. date: 2/13/2012

Contents

Acknowledgments

My deepest appreciation to my beautiful wife Courace, who inspired, encouraged and believed in me during this process. To my wonderful parents Neville and Shernette Fisher who provided a nurturing, supportive and godly environment for me to flourish and grow. I am so proud of you both. Thank you Mom and Dad! To my aunt Jonie Reid for your support and prayers. Special thanks to Bishop Frank Otto and wife, Apostle Felix Samuels and wife, Overseer Valvern Wittock and wife, Dr. Colin Cawley and wife, Evangelist Christopher Bryan and wife and others who have been a great source of encouragement and support. Finally, to my support team thank you for believing in this message and supporting me to publish it.

Preface

The title of this book is poignant in and of itself: *The Way Forward*. It denotes motion, specifically movement with a prescribed course or passage to greater progression and development—in this case, spiritually. But the arduous challenges and vicissitudes of life have sadly rendered some immobile or in a backslidden position. In some cases, these pressures have subjected many to a labyrinthine state of going 'round and 'round, with no sense of direction. As such, this book was inspired by and written to the passionate believer who has become lost in life's maze of pressures, hardships, and strains. The aim, then, is to explore biblical truths to gain spiritual development and maturity. It is also designed to unearth the challenges within the church world in a penetrating and provocative manner.

At this juncture in the Christian experience, there is a need for those who have been called by God to begin pointing the church in the right direction. John 14:6 gives us a glimpse of the fundamental principle for moving forward. The Scripture points out that Jesus declared, "...I am the way, the truth, and the life: no man cometh unto the Father, but by me." (John 14:6) Clearly Jesus is the course or the way that will lead to truth and ultimately life!

The Scriptures go on further to explicitly demarcate that the broad and narrow roads lead to two separate destinations. As such, there can be no confusion that these two roads are diametrically opposite in course and outcome. Therefore, if there is ever a time that a beacon needs to be lit, it is now — a beacon that will illuminate the mind and method of God for these very challenging times.

This book is designed to ignite a renewed passion for God and the establishment of His Kingdom on the earth. Thus, as you read through the pages of this book, it is my prayer that it will challenge you to confront the raw reality of the season and at the same time lead you to deeper prayer life. Not only that, but I pray that you will become militant and resolute in being an active participant in building the Kingdom of God.

Last, to get the most out of this book, I encourage you to search and meditate upon all of the Scriptures cited. As you are faithful, God will surely build into you a new love for Him as well as for the church — a renewed desire to see it established as a place of refuge in these last days. May the blessings of heaven rest on you as you read through these pages!

Introduction

Confused? Frustrated? Afraid? Perplexed? Today this has become the prevailing condition of many. This diagnosis is no longer confined to the world but has seeped into the church. As a matter of fact, every facet of people's lives are being challenged to the point that many have resorted to suicide, cigarettes, legal and illegal drugs, spirits, and other forms of addictions in hopes of drowning it out. The collapse of the markets and the increase of sickness, crime, and natural disasters have amplified this sense of hopelessness and despair. Being overshadowed with unfortunate external and internal pressures and occurrences, many have lost direction and any sense of what to do next. Amid dealing with insurmountable odds, as we are today, it is imperative that we stop, regroup, and reevaluate where we are and whether or not we are stagnant, regressing, or progressing.

In the summer of 2000, while on a visit to England, I was deeply concerned about the state of the church and where she is heading. Based upon observation, it dawned on me to ask where the passion and dedication for the ministry are. When will we be united for the ultimate purpose of winning souls for Christ and disrupting the enemy's plans? Where is the manifestation of the power that should be evident when God's people come together? Confronted with these concerns, I became somewhat despondent and ventured to seek answers to these questions from senior people of like, precious faith. However, after having a few conversations, I was not satisfied with the answers provided. I immediately sought God, and thoughts began to flow through my spirit as I wondered, *Where do we go from here?* I began to put pen to paper as the Holy Spirit led me to write concerning the way forward.

Clearly, there are rules of the road that one must adhere to in order to operate a motor vehicle. Even before someone is issued a driver's license, he or she has to undergo an examination. This examination is to determine whether the potential driver has the required knowledge to operate the vehicle. The knowledge allows the driver to effectively operate the vehicle and interpret and understand signs, maps, and so on. God has provided us with the vehicle to move with Him. The Bible is the road map to get us to the point of fruitfulness and ultimately into His rest. The Bible, then, is much more than a good book we occasionally dust off and read. It is the sole source to get one from a state of hopelessness, confusion, despair, fear, and so on. In other words, the purpose of the word of God is to poise and position man in the way forward. Moving forward will bring one to the destination of being in God's presence!

My desire is that *The Way Forward* will stimulate us to examine our current position(s) or status as believers and the state of the church as we experience it today. The content emphasizes the soulful plea of the called-out believer(s) for the return to holiness as delineated by God because the church is positioned for the most crucial stage of the church experience—the Lord's coming!

The Way Forward is intended to motivate the believer not to accept spiritual mediocrity as the norm but to embark on a spiritual journey with the Lord, meeting all the requirements as outlined in the Word. Whether you are a leader or a layperson, it's my desire that this book will challenge you to become the vessel God intended you to be from the beginning of time. Hopefully this book will be a gauge as to where one may be in God's economy and will spiritually awaken and bring the thirsty soul to a higher level of consciousness. The central message of this book is simple—move forward and refuse to become stagnant or motionless!

Chapter One

Take a Moment to Consider

> When I consider thy heavens, the work of thy fingers, the moon and the stars, which thou hast ordained; What is man, that thou art mindful of him? and the son of man, that thou visitest him?
>
> — Psalm 8:3-4

The clamor, noise, stress, and strain of life can make it so difficult to stop and enjoy. So many times, the unrelenting pace of life and the instant mind-set has made it almost impossible to stop and smell the roses! This nonstop wave of progression has plunged its fangs in the lives of countless millions, and as a result, it has revolutionized the way we live—"on the go." In light of this, I have heard too often the complaint, "I don't even have time to think!" The pressure of life has so many in a headlock, suffocating them from understanding and fulfilling their purpose and experiencing happiness. Along with that, time itself has become a formidable foe that has heightened this standoff. But if you had a moment to consider something, what would it be?

Have you ever stopped to consider the grandeur and splendor of the celestial terra firma or the innumerable angelic hosts or the serenity of this place? Or have you just pondered the extent of God's limitless power as He created man from the dust of the earth and how the body is really a display of wonder and intricate detail? Or have you pondered why God, in His infinite love and mercy, selected you from billions of people? Have you wondered what it was in God's mind that made you stand out from so many others? Really, have you just stopped and wondered in the sheer amazement of why?

David in Psalm 80:4 asked God this poignant question, "What is man that thou art mindful of him and the son of man?"

David, in his pursuit to understand, questioned God by juxtaposing the splendor and radiance of the heavens to the insignificance of man. But after conversing with God, David remained awestruck as to why God is so cognizant of sin-prone man and his actions and affairs. The Psalmist then was left to worship and observe with wonder the infinite mercies of God.

Like David, we need to take periodic moments in our lives where we just stop and consider. David's moment to question God and His enthrallment of man is an example for us to follow. It is a starting point for movement—forward!

Love that Moved God!

Fostering any relationship can be a daunting experience. In the relationship between God and His creation, He made the first move, showcasing His immeasurable love and admiration for us. John 3:16 puts it this way:

> For God so loved the world, that he gave his only begotten Son, that whosoever believeth in him should not perish, but have everlasting life.

The price Jesus paid on Calvary was not the simple action of trying to woo mankind. It was the purest declaration of His unfailing and limitless love to us. First John 4:9-10 conveys God's heart and admiration to man this way:

> In this was manifested the love of God toward us, because that God sent his only begotten Son into the world, that we might live through him. Herein is love, not that we loved God, but that he loved us, and sent his Son to be the propitiation for our sins.

God, through Jesus Christ, became the ultimate sacrifice to break the curse of sin that tore the bond between God and man. Without question, the infinite suffering of Jesus to bring man back into fellowship with Him goes far beyond any human parent or spouse. This is certainly the greatest love story known to man!

If you or I were in a relationship with someone for any length of time, there would be an expectation that the level of communication established would enhance the union of the parties involved—agreed? This law is true in both the natural and the supernatural. Once one has developed that intimate relationship with God, the outcome and experience are wondrous. For so long, many have believed that attending or participating in church is the sum total of one's experience with God.

Sadly, this erroneous concept has strongly pervaded Christendom. Actually, the experience of knowing and serving God goes far beyond the confines of the four walls of a church building. There is so much more of God that we have yet to tap into. Unfortunately, the experience of church as it pertains to what happens within a building has placed limitations in how we perceive and understand God.

Consider Your Position. Are You Stagnant?

> I know thy works, that thou are neither cold nor
> hot: I would thou wert cold or hot.
>
> So then because thou art lukewarm, and neither
> cold nor hot, I will spue thee out of my mouth.
>
> — Revelation 3:15–16

Stagnation: *a state of inactivity, being stagnant, standing still, without current or circulation (www.thefreedic-
tionary.com).*

Kahlil Gibran, a Lebanese American novelist, emphatically
declared, "March on. Do not tarry. To go forward is to move
toward perfection. March on, and fear not the thorns, or the
sharp stones on life's path." Certainty life experiences or circumstances and external worldly influences can aid in dimin-
ishing and hindering our consciousness for spiritual growth.
As easily as these challenging occurrences happen in one's
life, negative emotions or feelings can grab hold, and without
realization, one can slide into discontentment and abject despair. The outcome is spiritual stagnation, which has the insidious ability to siphon one's desire for God, and as a result,
barriers of frustration, discontentment, fear, denial, and anger
are constructed.

Revelation 3:15–16 gives us a view into God's thoughts on
spiritual stagnation. Although the primary purpose for
John's letters to the seven churches of Asia Minor was to give
God's report card of their spiritual condition, it also describes
the seven types of churches. Clearly John's writings to the
churches of Asia Minor have significant pertinence to us today. It is a direct warning not only to the church at large but
also to us on a personal level. It should propel us to consider
our personal walk with God. Am I lukewarm? Am I grow-

ing spiritually? Am I truly matching up to the word of God? Do my daily actions and disposition reflect and demonstrate spiritual growth?

These are very important questions that each of us needs to consider in our daily walk with the Lord. We can quite easily become so caught up in the experience of church that we lose sight of our personal relationship with the Lord. Unfortunately, many have equated the church experience as the sum total of their personal experience with God, but God is so desirous for greater communion and for us to be His disciples and follow after His precepts.

Recently, in my personal devotion I wondered to myself whether or not I was experiencing the awesomeness of God as I should. In those moments of reflection, I was confronted with the following questions from the Lord:

- Have I allowed life's challenges to cripple me so that I am unable to move forward in God?

- Why are we not seeing the occurrence of miracles on a greater scale?

- Why is there seemingly a lack of direction within the church in the twenty-first century?

After being confronted with such challenging questions, my response was personal introspection and repentance. This unrelenting burden to see God move changed my outlook on ministry in such a radical way. The weight of this burden stirred me to the point of evaluating the personal challenges I faced and what steps I took to ensure my spiritual vitality.

Realign Your Focus

At some point or another in our annual doctors' visits, our physicians will check our eyes to determine their health. Generally doctors will request the patient to focus his or her eyes on a distant screen and identify the numbers, and letters to determine the eyes' current condition. Focus is required for this assessment to be effective. In the same vein, before we can take strides forward, we must first consider where we are now. What does it take to move forward in God?

One of the key elements that is essential is the ability to focus on God and what He deems vital for spiritual growth and development. Isaiah 26:3 exhorts, "Thou wilt keep [him] in perfect peace, [whose] mind [is] stayed [on thee]: because he trusteth in thee."

There are times, though, when life's challenges can cause us to lose focus, and chaos ensues. But Isaiah is underscoring that there is a connection between one's focus and one's peace. In other words, the mind that is centered and confident in God will not be agitated by the trials to which it may be subject, be they sickness, poverty, persecution, or rejection. It should also be noted here the condition of the mind: "whose mind is stayed on thee [God]." In other words, it is a mind that is fixed, rooted, grounded, and firmly persuaded in God. As such, we must discipline and develop ourselves to understand and perceive life's particular circumstances and troubles God's way. Otherwise we can be prone to lose complete focus and reliance upon God.

Daniel 3:1–3 is a portrait of unwavering focus and belief. Shadrach, Meshach, and Abednego were not moved by Nebuchadnezzar's decree to worship the golden image, even if it meant death as the final outcome. Their conviction and resolution is what is noteworthy here. Nebuchadnezzar's plea for them to reconsider did not change their response. They articulated with undeniable confidence:

> O Nebuchadnezzar, we are not careful to answer thee in this matter. If it be so, our God whom we serve is able to deliver us from the burning fiery furnace, and he will deliver us out of thine hand, O king. But if not, be it know unto thee, O king, that we will not serve thy gods, nor worship the golden image which thou hast set up.

It certainly takes sheer resolution and sound conviction even when faced with certain death not to compromise or change one's mind. The online dictionary definition for the word "focus" sums up the stance of the three Hebrew boys best, "maximum clarity or distinctness of an idea" (www. thefreedictionary.com). What was in the minds of these young men that kept them so committed to God in Babylon?

Another key point to moving forward is having the ability to see things through God's perspective. In Isaiah 55:8-9 it affirms it this way:

> For my thoughts are not your thoughts, neither are your ways my ways, saith the LORD. For as the heavens are higher than the earth, so are my ways higher than your ways, and my thoughts than your thoughts.

This Scripture clearly states that no man can ever comprehend the mind of God. God is infinitely beyond anything we can comprehend. This dichotomy is further emphasized through Isaiah's remarkable use of measurement or scale imagery of the heavens to the earth. In other words, man's inability to measure the heavens and the earth speaks of the polarity of the thoughts of God to those of man. In Romans 3:11, the Amplified Bible confirms it this way:

> No one understands [no one intelligently discerns or comprehends]; no one seeks out God.

Instinctively, it is just easier to accept what we can understand and prove. But what is foreign or unknown to us, we generally have the tendency to dispel or disregard as truth. But if we were in the same situation as the three Hebrew boys, would our focus shift to compromise or despair, causing us to lose our ability to be (spiritually) objective? This could magnify or blow the problem out of proportion.

I am certain, that at one point or another we have been faced with problems that seemed mammoth or bigger than they actually were. All common sense and godly reliance went through the window. The problem seemed greater than God at the time. Why is it at the points of trouble or testing that we lose godly objectivity? Why do we seem to forget that problems have the ability to paralyze us within the immediacy of the circumstance?

Again, there is a principle that must be considered in the lives of the three Hebrew boys and even Daniel in Babylon. Their conviction and commitment to God gave them the courage to thrive despite the challenges of living in a heathen society. The Scriptures clearly show their unshakeable resolve even at the pain of death or the attempt to change identity as means to convert them. The fervency of their love for God surpassed the various tests they endured in Babylon.

If one is unable to see things God's way, then one may never feel inspired to seek after what is greater. There must be a personal yearning for the heart of God and an elevated spiritual scope to perceive and understand life. If we look at Enoch,

Abraham, and Noah, we see that they followed the voice of God — something they could not comprehended naturally. But they acted with sheer obedience and willingness even if it meant being criticized by their peers. Their desire for greater communion with God propelled them to move. As a matter of fact, the pursuit for God requires one to move.

Moving forward spiritually also involves emptying your mind and spirit of blockages or hindrances. Hebrews 12:1 instructs us this way:

> Let us lay aside every weight, and the sin which doth so easily beset us, and let us run with patience the race that is set before us ...

Paul uses the analogy of runners in the Greek games as an example of how we are to live as Christians. The hope of athletes is the reward of winning. Their strict concentration, tension, energy, and strenuous effort are the only means to obtain victory. The apostle Paul exhorts that this is the manner in which to run if we want to attain the reward.

Any successful runner knows that to minimize resistance, you must wear suitable clothing. Extra pounds, whether in body weight or clothes, impede speed and performance. In other words, to acquire victory, one must run "light." As the Scripture above says, "Let us lay aside every weight, and the sin which doth so easily beset us." Sin can generally be identified or recognized, and we know how to rightly respond — repent. Weights, on the other hand, can be deceiving, for they can be often obscured by well-intentioned motives. Emotional baggage, such as low-self esteem or guilt from past failures and disappointments, can be a weight that inhibits strides forward and ultimately victory.

Sometimes life can deal us blows that may cause us to become stuck or unmotivated to seek after God. Instead of us standing our ground, we resort to curling up, flight, and ultimately throwing in the towel. It is at these times when we must put on all our spiritual armor and prepare for battle. One battle at a time! One fight at a time! This is the kind of attitude we need to move forward. Once we have come to this spiritual understanding, our perspective begins to change. You begin to look deeply and further ahead to the next horizon. Mediocrity is no longer an acceptable spiritual experience.

Conversely, when we truly begin to view things God's way, then the next challenge we encounter will give us the drive to keep moving forward. The apostle Paul asserted the following after assessing his personal life hardships, trials, and insufficiency from the perspective of God:

> For I reckon that the suffering of this present time are not worthy to be compared with the glory which shall be revealed in us.
>
> Romans 8:18

The perspective that the many heroes of faith demonstrated must be something that we hold on to and follow. In so doing, it will give us the strategy of God to be victorious when challenged with circumstances. Looking forward, then, is not a mere option but is mandatory for one to achieve spiritual success.

In the words of a familiar proverb, "What you behold is what you become." This guiding maxim is not just a common theoretical prose, but found in its simple packaging are pearls of wisdom. Thus, it behooves us to consider that the abstract of the supernatural cannot be understood by the carnal mind. The things of the spirit require a spiritual mind to perceive and understand. Seeing things God's way will result in moving God's way, which is forward.

Consider the Conclusion of the Matter—Start Moving!

> For all this I considered in my heart even to declare
> all this ...

> —Ecclesiastes 9:1

In the conclusion of Solomon's life, he came to a stark point of revelation and penned some of the most poignant insights on how to live life. The Bible gives us a glimpse into the lavish lifestyle Solomon lived. It records that Solomon's set income alone was more than thirty tons of gold per year. It also goes on to highlight that Solomon's throne of ivory was overlaid with pure gold and was the most elaborate throne of any king in the world (2 Chronicles 9:17–19). These points do not fully capture the full extent of the grandeur and splendor that Solomon lived.

But after experiencing the wealth and finest of life, Solomon declared in Ecclesiastes 1:2, "Vanity of vanities, saith the Preacher, vanity of vanities; all is vanity."

It must be pointed out, though, that the word vanity as used in the Bible does not have the same meaning as we know today. Vanity in this book is translated to mean "emptiness" or "unsatisfactory" or "transitory" (passing away without continuance). So when Solomon was saying all is vanity, he was actually saying that nothing in the world is permanent or eternal, and as such, it cannot bring lasting satisfaction to man. Solomon went on further to proclaim:

> Then I looked on all the works that my hands had
> wrought, and on the labour that I had laboured

> to do: and, behold, all was vanity and vexation of
> spirit, and there was no profit under the sun.
>
> -Ecclesiastes 2:11

This point of revelation realigned Solomon's understanding to the purpose and intent for life. He also gave us a principle we should use to live life in communion with God. He affirms it this way in Ecclesiastes 12:13:

> Let us hear the conclusion of the whole matter: Fear
> God, and keep his commandments: for this is the
> whole duty of man.

Solomon's personal assessment of life clearly shows that true meaning or pleasure cannot be derived from possessions and status. But the conclusion of the matter, which is life, is to fear God and keep His commandments, and in so doing, true pleasure will ensue.

I believe whole-heartedly that this book of wisdom was designed to get one to consider the summation of life and come to a point of decision as to what is of true value. Is it worldly possessions and pleasures? Or is it fearing God and keeping His commandments?

For most Westerners, life is about attaining possessions. Daily we spend most of our waking hours working to earn money to acquire possessions. Then we devote more time and effort thinking about things we want to buy and how to earn more money. It is fascinating, though, that even homeless people have this same goal and seem to have an inordinate preoccupation with collecting things they push around in their shopping carts. This Western world dogma has painted the utopian picture that material possessions, power, and sex equate with a good life. As such, this worldly idealism has thwarted the minds and perspectives of so many, thus causing many to believe that their personal value is derived from their wealth, possessions, and power.

It is a sad commentary when we start using the base things of this world to bring value to who we are. How does the lesser thing become greater? Solomon's personal experience is a lived account for us to observe. "Wisdom is the principal thing; therefore get Wisdom: and with all thy getting get understanding." Proverbs 4:7 must be the banner by which we live! Wisdom is the actualization of knowledge. It is time to actualize what we know and move forward! Get up and move ...

Chapter Two

Get Rid of the Robbers

The thief cometh not, but for to steal, and to kill, and destroy: I am come that they might have life, and that they might have it more abundantly.

—John 10:10

The gospel of Matthew 24 is an explicit chapter that systematically highlights the nature of the end of time. It also captures the manner of person we are to be in light of this progressive move to the Lord's coming. Yet amid the warnings from the biblical writers, there has never been a time like the present where there is such an increase in confusion within the world and even Christendom. Few are sure about anything, and many Christians are floundering around with no sense of direction. As such, more and more people have lost their zeal and love for God and have become vulnerable to the ploys and schemes of the enemy.

To intensify this, we are experiencing some of the greatest levels of sociopolitical and spiritual unrest and turmoil ever experienced. National sovereignty, political reformation, morality, and the once-predictable global marketplace are no longer beacons of security and progression or hallmarks to follow. Rather, they have become capricious entities globally. Even amid the implosion within the economic and political structure, the world is at arms against terrorists who threaten the fundamental rights, freedoms, and liberties of human-kind. Similarly, the church has felt its debilitating blows both locally and at large. Even as the world is fighting this war against terrorism, the church is also fighting against "spiritual terrorists" who subvert doctrine, abort the gifts of the spirit, prophesy falsehoods, and divide churches.

Although we have acknowledged that these signs charac-terize the coming of the Lord, the question that needs to be asked is whether we have truly prepared ourselves for it. As a result, the enemy has intruded into our lives and has stolen our valuables, such as our innocence, confidence, faith, hope and passion. The palpable issues, such as our local church or world crises, to name a few, have become smoke screens that obstruct our view of the tactics of the enemy, which is to steal, kill, and ultimately destroy. We must be mindful of the seduc-tive schemes of the enemy. Similarly, a robber will observe his or her environment first and then select a potential victim or place to commit the crime. The devil employs the same tactic. We must be alert and conscious at all times. We can never let down our guard or become naïve to spiritual warfare.

I am certain that if I asked, "Is there anything too hard for God?" everyone would answer with a resounding no! Luke 1:37 affirms, "For with God nothing is ever impossible and no word from God shall be without power or impossible of fulfillment."

There will certainly be times in our lives when circumstances will back us into a corner, and it is at that point that the true test of our beliefs will come. Will I succumb to the pressure and respond ignorantly, or will I use godly wisdom and patience to attain victory? This is a question of importance, which was discussed in the earlier chapter.

There are many forms of expression that try to capture the human condition and spirit. It can come in the form of literature, art, or dance. Music is one of the central mediums through which we have been able to emote or express ourselves, particularly our triumphs, trials, hope(s) and dreams. As such there are countless songs with lyrical content that speak to self realization or revelation about the prescribe course of their lives. Mrs. E. E. Williams, a hymnologist, is a great example, and she penned these poignant words:

> I have made our choice forever; I will walk with Christ my Lord. Naught from Him my soul can sever while I'm trusting in His word. I the lonely ways have taken, rough and toilsome though it be; And although despised, forsaken, Jesus I will go through with thee.

Mrs. Williams's lyrical content captures one who came to the stark understanding through adversity that God is the sole person who can bring solace and victory. The lyrics of this song are insightful in that they dispel the notion that the Christian landscape is void of trouble but gives us the assurance that God will be with us through it all.

So easily we have forgotten that when going through our trials, they are designed to build our trust in the Almighty. First Peter 4:12 confirms, "Behold, think it not strange concerning the fiery trials which is to try you, as though some strange thing happened unto you."

In other words, we are not to be apprehensive about the trials we may face, but we are to grab hold to the words of the apostle and, "Think it not strange." Trials have come to prove us and build and strengthen our character. Therefore, trials have worth because they make us like Christ. They are not optional but are required for our Christian development and deployment.

In times of hard trials, we have to encourage ourselves like the Psalmist David. In Psalm 43:5 he expresses, "Why art thou cast down, O my soul? and why art thou disquieted within me? hope in God: for I shall yet praise him, who is the health of my countenance, and my God."

David checks himself and realigns his focus from his current circumstances to hope in God. Put differently, when all else fails, your hope must remain in God. From there David moves back to his purpose — to praise: "For I shall yet praise him." Note the word yet. Yet is a conjunction that is equivalent to "but" or "nevertheless." David tells himself, "Even in the midst of turmoil and sore hardship, I will praise God nevertheless!" We have to move to a point of "nevertheless" in our Christian journey.

In time, a test will come to examine whether we have applied the word of God to our lives, specifically to our situations. The word of God should not just be considered the mental acquisition of knowledge but must also be something we apply to our everyday life experience. David came to the realization and confirmed, "Thy word have I hid in my heart, that I might not sin against thee" (Psalm 119:11). King David came to the revelation that only the Word could help him in remaining in fellowship with God.

Psalm 33:4 affirms, "For the word of the LORD [is] right; and all his works [are done] in truth."

Isaiah 40:8 states, "The grass withereth, the flower fadeth: but the word of God shall stand for ever." From generation to generation, the word of God has proven infallible and relevant. First Peter 1:25 in the Amplified Bibles states it this way: "But the Word of the Lord [divine instruction, the Gospel] endures forever ..."

The Word must not just be a mere utterance but the foundation we stand upon. The Bible is filled with promises that we should declare and live by. There are numerous promises that are outlined throughout the canon Scripture that we may have considered to be invalid or irrelevant to us. But the redemptive work of the cross has given us this access to this timeless validity to use. It is imperative now that we take God at His word. Second Corinthians 1:20 tells us, "For all the promises of God in Him are Yea, and in Him Amen, to the glory of God through us."

Whatever God says must come to pass, and no person, power, or thing can block it. Isaiah 55:11 affirms that God's Word will not return void and must accomplish what it set out to do! This verse is not a cliché or blanket promise but is a stipulation. In other words, God's Word must accomplish — that is a guarantee! Sadly, we have allowed some robbers to enter into our spirit and to lodge there for so long that they have become one with who we are.

There are a number of evils that the Bible speaks a great deal about, which I have classified as robbers. Below I have listed five robbers we need to be mindful of. Too many times, though, these robbers listed below have been considered nothing to be alarmed about or people think they are of no real threat or consequence to us. But they are serious and cannot be attached to the believer. That is why we need to examine these robbers more carefully.

Robber One—Fear

Often, fear has been repackaged as something that is not a serious vice to the believer; when in fact, it has a serious and deadly influence on the spiritual success of the believer. Fear is not our friend! A useful acronym to define fear is *False Evidence Appearing Real*. This is a definition I heard that captures this spirit succinctly. Second Timothy 1:7 exhorts, "For God hath no given us the spirit of fear; but of power, and of love, and of a sound mind."

The word for fear in this verse is not speaking about general fear as it is commonly called. The word fear in the Greek language is *deilias*, which means "cowardice" (Strong 1995). In other words, God has not given us a spirit of cowardice.

The Scripture brings up important points that we must consider. First, it points out that fear is a spirit. Second, it says that fear is a spirit that God did not give us. Fear is much more than just an emotion; it is a spirit. First John 4:18 states, "There is no fear in love; but perfect love casteth out fear: because fear hath torment. He that feareth is not made perfect in love."

There is no fear in love. Love is not an emotion that produces fear. Fear is tormenting in that it is a painful and a distressing emotion. It is a spirit that has been sent out by the devil, our enemy. The Bible declares in Ephesians 6:12:

> For we wrestle not against flesh and blood, but against principalities, against powers, against the rulers of the darkness of this world, against spiritual wickedness in high places.

This spirit oftentimes is not considered a formidable foe that can cripple the destiny and the purpose of the believer. For example, many suffer from the fear of death, poverty, sickness, and the uncertainty of the future. All of these apprehensions are examples that many contend with, thus suggesting that the love of God has not been perfected within them. When our love is perfected, we understand that God is in control of everything and there is nothing to be apprehensive or fearful about. If we are afraid, our minds are not well balanced as God describes. We fall into the category of a double-minded man as outlined in James 1:8. It is important to emphasize that fear is nothing to play with. In Revelations 21:8 it gives us a list of those that will not enter into eternal life.

> But the fearful, the unbelieving, and the abomin-
> able, and murderers, and whoremongers...

Robber Two—Unbelief

The Greek dictionary defines unbelief as "unfaithfulness" or "the state or quality of not believing; incredulity or skepticism, especially in matters of doctrine or religious faith" (Strong 1995). Simply put, unbelief is when one refuses to believe what God's Word outlines and subsequently fails to adhere to or follow what it tells us to do. Unbelief then is interconnected with disobedience, and it leads to other evils. Interestingly, the modern dictionary generally defines unbelief as something that is principally concerned with "religious matters." In essence, then, having unbelief in God is comparable to being in an adulterous affair. This is how God described Israel in the Old Testament when they fell into unbelief and idolatry.

Therefore, unbelief stands as an act of disrespect to the word of God because it questions the ability and working(s) of God. The Bible emphatically declares that God is sovereign and almighty. God can do anything but fail. The very handiworks of God in nature and even our personal well-being and health show forth the might and creative genius of God.

Unbelief can cause us not to experience the miraculous move of God. It shows us only opposition and negativity. In Mark 6:5, Jesus returned to His home country and on the Sabbath began to teach in the synagogue. Mark goes on further to record that many were astonished with His sayings. But Jesus could do no miracles because of their unbelief. Whenever unbelief is present, there can be no manifestation or act of God!

We can no longer aid and abet unbelief in our spirit. It will inhibit our spiritual growth. Unbelief does not have any reasoning ability. It causes you to have a spiritual mind-set that is one dimensional. For example, it is like some people who are never on the team of possibility rather the team of pessimism. Unbelief is an insidious spirit that aims to cripple the manifest move of God. This spirit must be bound and cast out!

Robber Three—Doubt

Oftentimes unbelief and doubt are considered synonymous or the same thing, but there are differences between the two. In the gospels, Jesus spoke at length about doubt. Jesus said that doubt affects one's ability to receive of God as one should. The Greek dictionary defines doubt as to "waver and hesitate." The modern English dictionary states that it is to "be uncertain about; consider questionable or unlikely; hesitate to believe and to distrust. To doubt as established is to be uncertain about something" (Mouton 1978). Perhaps it is something that causes one to question or to wrestle with how it could be. In essence, it causes one to doubt a specific fact or something of that nature. The distinction between doubt and unbelief is that the state of unbelief is to assert that a decision has been reached about something and that it could not have happened and it is just not possible that it is true. Put differently, doubt is a matter of the mind while unbelief is a matter of the heart. Doubt, then, is one's inability to understand what God is doing and why He is doing it.

Unfortunately, many have to see in order to believe like doubtful Thomas. John 20:24–29 captures the post-resurrection time of Jesus and Thomas's doubtful reaction:

> The other disciples therefore said unto him, We have seen the LORD. But he said unto them, Except I shall see in his hands the print of the nails, and put my finger into the print of the nails, and thrust my hand into his side, I will not believe. And after eight days again his disciples were within, and Thomas with them: then came Jesus, the doors being shut, and stood in the midst, and said, Peace be unto you. Then saith he to Thomas, Reach hither thy finger, and behold my hands; and reach hither thy hand, and thrust it into my side: and be not faithless, but believing. And Thomas answered and said unto him, My LORD and my God. Jesus saith unto him, Thomas because thou hast seen me, thou hast believed; blessed are they that have not seen, and yet have believed.

Thomas is similar to many of us at some point or another in our Christian walk. We have succumbed to wanting tangible proof in order to believe. It is important to remember that Thomas was one of Jesus's disciples. As a disciple, he witnessed miracle after miracle and sat and heard the prolific and didactic teachings of Jesus. Yet in spite of having such firsthand divine encounters with Jesus, Thomas was still unable to believe without seeing.

Thomas is an example for us so we will not fall into the same trap of requiring quantifiable facts. The wisdom of this world has contributed to our doubtful disposition at times. But God, through His Word, has left us a record of the supernatural power of God: the opening of the Red Sea and the Jordan River, raising Lazarus from the dead, and opening the eyes of the blind, to name a few.

It is important that we begin to speak life into our situations. For example, the woman in 2 Kings 4:23 whose son was dead, her declaration was, "It is well," in spite of her devastation about his death. Even in the face of hardship, we have to develop a divine assurance in God and a speech that reflects it. Proverbs 18:21 says, "Death and life [are] in the power of the tongue: and they that love it shall eat the fruit thereof."

First Corinthians 2:19 consoles us that God has great things in store for us even amid the hardships or trials we encounter from time to time: "But as it is written, Eye hath not seen, nor ear heard, neither have entered into the heart of man, the things which God had prepared for them that love him."

We have to override this spirit. We must condition ourselves that the best is yet to come. In other words, we have to live with anticipation that better is on the way. Hardships and difficulties may seem the norm, but if we believe that God has greater, we will receive it! Psalms 30:5 confirms, "Weeping may endure for a night, but joy cometh in the morning." Midnight is but for a few moments, and joy is promised in the morning!

Robber Four—Condemnation

Many believers battle with condemnation to the point that it has become an intrinsic part of their daily routine. Condemnation means to express strong disapproval or censure or to demonstrate guilt. It can also be associated with self-inflicted fault finding, guilt, or shame. Consequently, there are a number of things that can cause this response or disposition. It can be because of past failures, low self-esteem and traumatic occurrences. Oftentimes the church world has inadvertently inferred a concept of spiritual perfection that is often associated with works. Thus, it causes many to fall into this subtle trap of not measuring up to standards that are oftentimes paraded and praised within a church assembly.

Condemnation is a tactic of the enemy to thwart God's perspective of us, and as a result, it cripples the believer into a state of low self-esteem, guilt, or shame. In Romans 8:1 Paul exhorts the Roman brethren, "[There is] therefore now no condemnation which are in Christ Jesus, who walk not after the flesh, but after the Spirit."

Condemnation is a ploy of the enemy to minimize the inherent power of the believer. John 8:36 tells us, "If the Son therefore shall make you free, ye shall be free indeed."

John is reminding us that once Christ makes us free, we are free indeed. We are free, with no attachments or fine print. We are just free. But if we choose to live with guilt, it can eat away at our confidence, joy, and freedom, which salvation offers. In addition, it causes us to be in a state of spiritual weakness and depression. This will give the enemy a foothold to try and paralyze our ability to progress in God. It is vital for us to remember that God has made us kings and priests unto God (Revelations 1:6). Condemnation is always contrary to what God states in His Word about us. We must come to the point of acceptance and say, "I will not walk in condemnation because of this."

Robber Five—Intimidation

Intimidation is the act of forcing a weaker person to do something or making him feel afraid or timid. An analogy that fits this spirit is a puppet master who has another person on a string, thus controlling or manipulating his or her actions. In many cases, the intimidator totally affects what the victim is able or unable to do. For example, the intimidator may even dictate when one can praise and worship the Lord, where one goes, and how one gets there.

This is one of the main characteristics of the spirit of Jezebel. This particular spirit is operating with great intensity in these last days. It is manifesting itself globally. As such, the spirit of Jezebel is not a simple spirit; it a ruling-class spirit. The book of Revelation also captures the licentious and captivating power of this ruling-class spirit. Jezebel, the Phoenician queen of Israel and priestess of Baal, is considered one of the most wicked women of the Bible. First Kings 21:25 records that King Ahab was the weak-willed husband of Jezebel and that she dominated and led him to do much evil. Her domination of her husband is linked to all of Israel falling into idolatry. The spiritual decline of Israel led to God's judgment through famine. The prophet Elijah confronted this idolatry and killed Jezebel's false prophets of Baal on Mount Carmel. When Jezebel heard this, she threatened to take the life of Elijah. The prophet who had raised the dead and called down fire ran like a scared rabbit and became depressed because of Jezebel's power of intimidation. It must be underscored that this spirit is not simple in nature and cannot be something that is accepted. The power of intimidation is at the root of why many believers refuse to do what the Lord has told them to do.

Reject and Cast Out the Robbers

Jesus stated, "And he did not many mighty works there because of their unbelief" (Matthew 13:58). Sadly, so many believe God for everybody else and not for themselves. It is high time that we started believing for ourselves. The slogan "practice what you preach" must be something that we apply to our personal lives. Mark 6 is a case study for us to observe. The Bible records that Jesus could not perform any miraculous works, specifically healing the sick, because the house that He was in was filled with unbelief. In order for the miraculous to occur, Jesus had to dismiss those who carried unbelief. Put plainly, there are times when there are spirits that must be put out for God to move. This account highlights that Jesus had to remove the unbelievers. Anywhere these robbers are, the power of God is limited.

The book of Jude outlines that God destroyed many because of their unbelief. The Bible catalogs account after account where the power of God could not flow because of hindrances, such doubt or disbelief, which in turn caused a disconnection to the power of God.

We have to use the authority God has given and step out in faith. I believe wholeheartedly in the inherent power of the church. The book of Acts demarcates the manifest power and workings of the church. The church is a powerful and spiritual entity in the world. As believers, Mark 16:17 promises us, "These signs must follow them that believe." It is important to note, though, that there is a condition for this. You must believe! If there is no belief, no signs can follow. The Pauline writings go further and reveal to us that the five-fold ministry was left for us to operate. Once we come to this understanding that God has equipped us and we accept it, things must happen. As such, this generation is longing and waiting for the sons of God to arise. This is the time and season for the manifestation of the sons of God.

It is time now for believers to be mindful of their associations. If your associations are negative, contentious, jealous, unbelievers, Proud and intimidating, stay away! As believers, we have to be spiritually cautious of our affiliations. If we are not careful, we can easily fall prey to the subtle suggestions or their advances until eventually our spiritual wealth is stolen from us. Therefore, we cannot compromise or be passive; we must drive these robbers or spirits out. In other words, an eviction notice must be served to the robbers. This cannot be a point of negotiation but an absolute eviction! We have to define and declare to the enemy that there is no vacancy and they must leave. From a spiritual standpoint, we have the authority to dismiss the occupancy of these robbers. As expressed earlier, these robbers will damage and ultimately destroy us if we do not evict them!

Evict the Robbers and then Expect the Extraordinary!

We are living at an extraordinary moment in the body of Christ. The manifestation of the power of God must be evident among us. The acts of God were not restricted to recipients in the book of Acts or to the prophets of old. If we are going to see the tremendous move of God, we have to cut off the heads of these robbers once and for all. We must not repeat or mimic the children of Israel who were destroyed in the wilderness because of their unbelief and idolatry. It is high time that we became spiritually sober and cognizant. We can no longer meander in an aloof or immature position. We have to walk by faith and not by sight to lay hold to the miraculous.

The School of Seeking God

Our relationship with God is based upon covenant. Anything God ties Himself to or embraces, He cannot reverse. The writer of the Hebrews states clearly, "For he that cometh to God must believe that he is and that he is a rewarder of them that diligently seek him."

In Hebrews 11:6, the operative phrase is "diligently seek Him." This means a constant and tireless effort in going after and accomplishing something, specifically the pursuit of God. I believe this is the formula to find our way back to God, thus resulting in a victorious life and ultimately moving forward in God.

We need every child of God to enlist in the school of seeking God. This can be a very lonely experience because of the level of sacrifice required to achieve a tangible relationship with the Lord. This school of seeking is not very popular among most Christians today given the requirements. Within this school, we have to be willing and ready to give up our will and allow God to shape and mold us, which can be a painful and uncomfortable experience. Many Christians want spiritual growth to come in the easiest of ways, but it will cost something. The central question that must be answered is whether we are willing to pay the price.

It should also be emphasized that the school of seeking God calls for separation, consecration, determination, elevation of faith, and total dependence upon God. Unfortunately, there seems to be a lack of consistency as it pertains to seeking the Lord. Believers' passion for going after God has somehow been sidelined by their preoccupation with other things, resulting in a decline of a healthy spiritual appetite for God by so many Christians.

We can only go forward by searching for and believing the truth. John 14:6 denotes the epicenter to gaining truth. If we are to fulfill the mandate God has given us, we must honor His words, and we will be amazed to experience the power of God through revelation and miracles. Ephesians 4:28 pronounces, "Let him that stole steal no more: but rather let him labour, working with [his] hands the thing which is good, that he may have to give to him that needeth."

We can no longer allow the enemy to steal or invade our lives. Being a regular victim of spiritual robbery has to be something of the past. Our spiritual mindset has to be elevated to the point that we become diligent and defiant to the whims and tactics of the devil. Arguably, Hollywood's portrayal of the devil may have thwarted our perspective of his true nature and intent. The devil cannot be reasoned with or be swayed to become good. His aim is pure and complete evil. That is why we must come to the understanding that God has invested treasures in us, and we must remain watchful of the adversary's agenda — to kill, steal, and destroy!

Chapter Three

Politics and the Church

The plan of the enemy is strategic and calculated. Nothing is done haphazardly or by chance. Every move has a specific reason to garner a specific result! It is like a skilled chess player using careful precision in determining each move with the ultimate aim of being the victor. As such, failure or defeat is not an outcome the enemy is willing to settle for. Thus, the enemy will use unconventional and unexpected tactics to gain the upper hand and ultimately the victory.

History has shown time and again that our adversary is cunning and sly. His devices and tactics cannot be perceived from human intellect and reasoning. At one point, persecution, which was one of the primary means to pressure and stop the church, it's not longer the only means used by the devil. Subtlety is the ploy that the devil is using with great accuracy in this hour. Now the ideologies and systems of the world have slowly and ever so slightly interwoven themselves into the fabric of the church experience to the point where there is no distinction between them, and this has become accepted as the norm. In the upcoming chapter, we will examine the church and that it is a glorious entity that is unspotted from the world.

The supernatural nature of the church demands leadership that rises above humanistic perspectives. William E. Sangster lamented, "The church is painfully in need of leaders." Too many times leadership is viewed as the product of simply natural endowment, personality and intellectual acumen. It cannot be denied that such traits and scholastic attainment do enhance leadership, but such characteristics are not of paramount importance in the scope of a spiritual leader. One writer put it this way: "The real qualities of leadership are to be found in those who are willing to suffer for the sake of objectives great enough to demand their wholehearted obedience" (Sanders 1980). In other words, any leader that is going to be used of God must be obedient in every sense of the word.

It needs to be reinforced that God's chosen leaders are not made by election or appointed by men. Only God can make a man — in this case a God-centered leader! Sadly, simply holding a position in church does not constitute one as a leader who is God approved and selected.

Lets examine the church more closely. The church is a glorious entity that is unspotted from the world. It is a spiritual institution established and ruled by God. No person can take ownership or credit for its establishment or longevity. It is a theocratically ruled entity that will never be relinquished or overthrown.

It is surprising to discover that in the King James Version of the Bible, the term "leader" occurs only six times, three of which are singular and three times in a plural way. This does not mean that this theme is not of prominent importance. Usually it is referred to in different terms, the most common being "servant." You will notice in Numbers 12:7 that it is not "Moses the leader," but rather "Moses, my servant."

If we truly evaluate the mantra of leadership today, we have lost sight of servanthood. This principle of serving others is no longer the propelling force behind our actions within the kingdom. We have succumb to the humanistic perspective of "me, myself, and I." As such, the vested power of serving others has gone. Jesus, in His discourse with His disciples, instructed them that to become the greatest of all, you must become a servant (Mark 9:44).

We have bypassed being a servant for greatness. How does one become great by being a servant first? This is a prevalent question that warrants an answer and greater examination by so many that operate within church today. But networking and devising personal strategies to move one to reach acclaim and recognition have thwarted the mindset of so many. Their central aim sadly is, "How can I get to greatness?" The prophetic writings of Isaiah elucidated the manner and spirit in which Jesus would come (Isaiah 42:1–5). You will note that Jesus voluntarily emptied Himself and concealed His splendor and power (Philemon 2:7). He voluntarily became a lowly servant, subjecting Himself to sinful flesh. Jesus is the prime example, showcasing to us that the requirement of ministry is serving. Ministry is not about personal aggrandizement of oneself, but it is purely about serving God and His people.

Theocracy Ruled out for a Monarchy

The Bible tells us that what was written before was written for our example (Romans 15:4 and 1 Corinthians 10:11). The story in the first book of Samuel is an example that must be explored to glean the interwoven truths that are applicable to us today. This account illustrates that when we consciously veer off course and follow the world and its system, it severs us from God and His precepts, plan, and purpose.

The first book of Samuel tells the story of Israel's transition from a theocracy, or state ruled by God, to a monarchy, or state ruled by a political leader. *The Christian Today Bible Dictionary's* definition of theocracy will provide further clarity to the process of Israel's spiritual decline:

> Theocracy is a word that was first used by Josephus which denotes that the Jewish people were under the direct government of God himself. That meant that the nation of Israel was subjected to the will of their invisible King—Jehovah. And as such the nation was His servants and HE ruled over their public and private affairs by communicating to them His will through the prophets. In essence, they were the subjects of a heavenly, not of an earthly, king. They were Jehovah's own subjects, ruled directly by Him.

> *Christian Today Bible Dictionary,* 2011

The Bible clearly tells us that Israel started out as a nation with tribes led by priests or other religious officials. First Samuel 8 and 9 unveils how Israel became a nation-state led by a centralized king. First Samuel 8 outlines that the elders of Israel gathered before Samuel, the God-appointed leader, and declared, "Thou art old and thy sons walk not in thy ways: now *make us a king to judge us like all the nations*" (1 Samuel 8:5). Although their request seems logical, that the rule of a single king would bring a sense of unity and cohesiveness to Israel, the opposite was the case. Israel's desire to be like the other nations and their blatant rejection of a God-ruled nation was problematic. These leaders must have felt they were suggesting a course of action that would benefit the nation. But their reasoning was void of God's perspective. Their rejection of God birthed the governance of a man-made, man-led, man-controlled nation—a system that was not fully ruled by the Almighty. Arguably this was one of the carefully devised moves of the enemy to shift God's people from theocracy to autocracy.

This rational action by the elders of Israel to employ a natural or man-ruled system is reminiscent of today. We have bought into the notion that we must be like the other nations of the world, and as such we have adopted the concept of making decisions for God's people without His consultation or approval.

This scriptural text also highlights God's ambivalence regarding the monarchy, which escalates this conflict. On one hand, God and Samuel were displeased at Israel's demand for a king because God was the central ruler. As such Israel's refusal to believe in God spoke to their distrust that God's religious laws were inadequate to rule the people. Then on the flip side, God willingly chose Saul to be king, identifying Saul as the deliverer of his people. God then reconciled this contradiction by distinguishing Israel's status as a human institution from its status as a divine one. As this shift happened, Samuel warned Israel about the dangers of having a king—woes that could not be reversed. Have we become exactly like Israel and rejected God? The pivotal question that needs to be asked is how do we rule a God-created institution such as the church and leave God out of it? How do we devise natural governance for a spiritual entity?

It is important to highlight that there are consequences of moving away from a theocracy. Israel's move away from a God-appointed leader commenced the division of religious and political life in Israel. Similarly, this has begun to happen within the church—a divide because of church politics. This transition from Samuel represents the old rule of the judges and Saul as the new monarchy despite Saul's failed attempts.

This account demonstrates the confusion that erupts on how religion and politics ought not to entwine, which is the chief conflict in this chapter. We saw this conflict when Saul made the gravest mistake as king to carry out the sacrificial duties of the priesthood—a role exclusively given to men appointed by God! Sadly, we see this case is all too familiar within the church. Political affairs and control have become the thrust of the church experience, dictating how God's kingdom should be governed, rarely with consultation or approval from God. As a result, there is a divide and no glory to God!

As we examine this account further, each stage of this transition highlights another figure other than Samuel and Saul. But as much as God may bless the king, He will not allow him to commit the sorts of human errors and injustices that human rulers are prone to commit. This account teaches that Saul's demise as king was tragic in that he made what we may categorize as a small human mistake—disobedience.

At the heart of this disobedience was the tragic flaw of many heroes—Saul was more concerned with earthly possessions and human customs than with spiritual matters. Saul planned to present the plunder he took from the Amalekites as a sacrifice to God. In divine response to Saul's failure, 1 Samuel 15:10–14 unfolds in this way:

> Now the word of the LORD came to Samuel, saying, "I greatly regret that I have set up Saul as king, for he has turned back from following Me, and has not performed My commandments." And it grieved Samuel, and he cried out to the LORD all night. So when Samuel rose early in the morning to meet Saul, it was told Samuel, saying, "Saul went to Carmel, and indeed, he set up a monument for himself; and he has gone on around, passed by, and gone down to Gilgal." Then Samuel went to

> Saul, and Saul said to him, "Blessed *are* you of the
> LORD! I have performed the commandment of the
> LORD." But Samuel said, "What then *is* this bleat-
> ing of the sheep in my ears, and the lowing of the
> oxen which I hear?"

This shift from theocracy to autocracy or even democracy unveils the many dangers that a leader can find him or herself
in. Saul thought as he returned from annihilating the Amalekites that all was well. He boasted to Samuel of his obedience:
"I have performed the commandments of the Lord." But Samuel retorted, "What then is this bleating of the sheep in my
ears, and the lowing of the oxen which I hear?" Sadly, Saul
thought he had performed the commandments of the Lord
even though he willfully chose the degree of his obedience.
It is a frightening thing when we can determine the extent
of what we term obedience and then define it as following
the commandments of the Lord. Really, that is not obedience.
Obedience is not something that can be done partially; it requires total adherence.

The Bible tells us that Samuel pled to the Lord for Saul. But
God rejected him. There is a distinctive sound in the supernatural when one is obedient or disobedient. The prophetic
ear will hear it and ask, "What then is this bleating of the
sheep ...?" That question was not so much about the sheep as
it was to Saul's obedience. Saul, why did you not obey?

In Exodus 17:14 and Deuteronomy 25:19, the sentence of condemnation was pronounced on the Amalekites. Judgment
was certain. How many times have we boasted of obedience
to the command of God but instead have displayed the love
of the world, the indulgence of the flesh, and the disputation
and neglect of holy duties, just to name a few?

This story demonstrates the dangers of moving away from a theocracy. In moving away, we have spawned either an autocratic rule, that is a self-ruler, or democratic rule where the people rule. Both of these can have drastic implications on the church experience. We have many people who have become autocratic, believing they are lords over God's people. Their agenda is generally self-serving and self-seeking, not taking into consideration God's people. Then on the other end, we have churches that have opted to be run or ruled by the people. Thus, they create an environment that selects God's directives and plans as secondary. Both of these models have left us vulnerable to the stealth schemes of the enemy, and as such, we have seen the Devastating explosion and implosion within the church. Specifically, we have seen an exponential rise in disputation, wars, and conflicts leading to church splits, which have prevented so many from moving into the realm of the spirit.

Politics have been responsible for affecting so many within Christendom to the point that some believers have decided they will never get involved in leadership as a result of it. But we have to seek God for godly leadership that will embrace and follow His plans and precepts. For example, the building of the Tabernacle of Moses explicitly shows Moses built it according to God's pattern (Hebrews 8:5). Moses did not devise his own plan, nor did he tweak it with his own human ideas. Rather, he followed it completely as God specified. God is raising up a people who will not rely on human decision making void of seeking God but will endeavor to follow His precepts so the revealed purpose of God can be displayed.

Chapter Four

Leaders at Loggerheads

Disclaimer: *This chapter is not for weak-minded, faint-hearted, jelly-backed Christians. Rather, it is for the passionate Christian who will no longer tolerate mediocrity and the average church experience. It is also for the believer who is defiant of the schemes of enemy through disputation and disunity, which affects the laity's ability to move forward.*

From whence come wars and fightings [or fighting?] among you? Come they not hence, even of your lusts that war in your members?

—James 4:1

This chapter was very important for me to write and include within this book. I feel passionately that much attention must be placed on examining the effects of disunity within the church. All too often leadership has dismissed the entrenched woes that disunity imposes upon the laity, thus paralyzing their ability to move forward. As such, disunity can no longer be the elephant in our sanctuaries that we consciously disregard. It cannot be something that just gets swept under the carpet with the hopes that the cliché, that "time heals all wounds" will ring true. That is why disunity is a critical matter that needs to be explored further.

Disunity is the opposite of the model of salvation. One of the central objects of salvation is to reunite, bring together, and reconcile humankind back to God. As a model, then, we must endeavor to walk in the unity of spirit in the bond of peace as the Ephesians writer expounds in Ephesians 4:3.

*****

Human history has shown that no generation can rise above the level of their leadership. Nations rise and fall due to the effectiveness of their governments. Therefore, it is imperative that the women and men respond to the call of God and choose to become reliable leaders (Damazio, 2000). History has shown that the church has contended with issues of leadership failures. But God has shown that He will not allow the church to be sabotaged by the weakness and inability of man.

The apostle Paul is noted as one of the most prolific writers of the New Testament. Many biblical theologians are enamored with his ability to pen a letter that captured the spiritual condition of the church and yet still exhort them to come to the fullness God intended for them. There can be no denying that Paul's explicit and poignant instructions to the various churches of Asia Minor remain relevant to the church now. Without question this highlights the greatness of our God and the power of the proceeding word of God.

As one takes further consideration of these letters, it becomes apparent that they provide insight to godly leadership, the qualifications, and more importantly, the characteristics that were required for leaders then and today. Not only that, but it also clarifies the characteristics that are critical to the development of Christian leadership. That is why each of these letters attempts to address questions such as faith, marriage, unity, spiritual gifts, and so on to bring leadership and ultimately the church into divine alignment.

Leadership of the twenty-first century is certainly at loggerheads! Leaders today are inadvertently and intentionally positioned there. You may ask what loggerheads is. Loggerheads means quarrellings or to be at strife *(www.hyperdictionary. com)*. With this revival for doctrinal and directional change for the church, it has only amplified it.

Leadership within Christendom has seen an exponential rise in scrutiny and denigration. Sadly, we find both leaders and parishioners scrutinizing leadership. Like no other, this process of scrutiny has arguably contributed to much of the divisions and quarrellings that the apostle Paul and James warned of. We see in the book of Acts that circumcision was the first major issue that threatened to divide the church into a Jewish Christianity and non-Jewish (Gentile) Christianity. This issue was the focus of many of Paul's letters in the New Testament as he gave a passionate plea to his followers to have a single unified Christian faith with both Jews and Gentiles together as one faith and body. The result of this pending division over circumcision was the Council of Jerusalem, where the apostles met to decide the role of circumcision within Christianity.

The Whole Body

As far back in time as can be recalled, there have been many calls for unity within the church. Many sermons have been preached imploring members to embrace the strength of unity. The most poignant analogy used to achieve this goal is that of likening the church to the physical body. In Paul's address to the Ephesians brethren, he writes, "There is one body, and one Spirit, even as ye are called in one hope of your calling" (Ephesians 4:4).

There can be no mistaking that there is only one body! From the opening verse in Genesis to the concluding chapter of Revelation, we see the motif of "one" carried throughout the entire Bible. Numbers have significance within the Scriptures. Biblical numerology can be useful in that it can help us to get a deeper understanding to the purpose and plan of God. In this case, one is the number of God and independence is also attached to it as well. As such, it excludes all things that are different. This number also denotes meaning as it pertains to the beginning of things. Unity is generally synonymous with this number in that it stands alone and cannot be divided (Mitchell 2011). Therefore, the power of one is something that we must strive to achieve as believers.

The analogy of our body has a number of symbolic or analogical meanings as it pertains to the church and the believer. For example, if our fingertip hurts, our entire body registers that singular pain. In cases of that sort, one does not remove the finger that hurts in an effort to stop the pain and still expect to continue as normal! As understandable as this concept is, theoretically we are witnessing the dividing of Christ as a means to gain some of level of normalcy.

When division sets in, the power of God cannot be seen. If you examine the verses that follow, Paul is exhorting the Ephesians to come to unity of the faith. The upcoming chapter outlines that the church is a living organism. It is a spiritual entity on earth. This organism has a DNA code that produces specific identifiable characteristics. Man has tried to take ownership of it, but it is beyond human intellect and the ability of natural man to lord over. This erroneous concept, along with other things, has arguably led to the dysfunction and disunity we experience today.

Similarly, we should not expect to separate ourselves from those members who are hurting or who we perceive to be the cause of our hurt and still expect to be whole. We are all members of one body! Oddly, we have forgotten this. The enemy has distracted us with the trivial pursuits of "natural power," consisting simply of the people we can control, and as a result we have lost sight of the positional stance God had intended for us since the beginning. Like Eve, the laity have distracted us with half truths. Because of this, the enemy has shifted our focus, and consequently we have been rendered ineffective in dealing with hurting people within the world and church alike. Arguably, as long as we remain out of our God-ordained position, we leave ourselves vulnerable to the effects of what I term spiritual HIV.

In the interchange of disunity and dysfunction, we have over-looked the fact that such actions affect others. This debilitating effect of disunity is transmitted to our children. There is a popular saying, "Children live what they learn and learn what they live." If a child constantly sees his or her parents feuding, he or she will accept this behavior or action as normal and as an acceptable way to behave. Unless he or she accepts positive influences outside of the home, he or she is likely to carry the same negative, cantankerous characteristics through to adulthood.

Within the church, our leaders may be likened to parents. The laity, which we classify the children, may begin to mimic, consciously or subconsciously, the qualities that are outstanding in their leaders. Hence, as long as our leaders are at loggerheads, the spirit of antagonism will pervade the rest of the church, and the body will remain disjointed and will never function at the full capacity God intended. When there is no unity, it weakens the spiritual immunity of the assembly, and it becomes susceptible to foreign elements.

One of the glorious aspects of the church is her ability to transcend appetites and in her strength to bring streams of revival that transform individuals, communities, and countries. In the past, all the great revivals were born out of a divine move of God to bring unity to the body. However, in this generation the local assembly has contracted a fatal virus that has the ability to threaten its vitality.

This disease is comparable to HIV, which breaks down the immune system, thus exposing the body and in this case the church or local assembly to viruses and or foreign agents to the body. One of the prevalent viruses is *"disunity* and *division,"* which sets leaders against leaders and parishioners against parishioners. Arguably, many of the mechanisms that have generated this division within the church are frivolous and trite in nature. The devil, the accuser of the brethren, has amplified these small things until they have grown to sizeable proportions.

As I further examined the symptoms and conditions of HIV, I made a startling discovery that this disease attacks the central organs of the body until it eventually leads to death. That is why a background understanding of this disease needs to be explained in more depth so we can get a clearer picture of the dynamics happening within the spiritual world concerning the body of Christ.

It is important to note that people living with HIV may feel and look completely well, but their immune systems are nonetheless damaged, in many cases beyond recovery. Once someone is infected he or she has the ability to pass on the HIV virus immediately, despite his or her healthy disposition. As time passes without effective treatment, HIV weakens the infected person's immune system, making him or her much more vulnerable to opportunistic infections, such as the flu, colds, etc. These infections are caused by germs that are around us all the time and can be normally fought off by a healthy immune system. Once HIV has broken down the body's defenses, such infections can take hold and produce any of a wide range of symptoms, some of which can be very severe, such as certain cancers, and become more common when the immune system is weakened.

Like HIV, once foreign agents such as disunity and pride have free course within the church body, the result is the weakening of the fabric and flow of the Holy Spirit. As such, the local church's ability to defend itself and to detect what is of God wanes. The devil may be able to get us to believe that because we look okay or feel okay at the present, everything is fine even though disunity is at an all-time high.

The case study of Joshua and Achan is a point for observation in that a breach, or in this case a foreign agent, affects everyone. This account highlights what happens when something or someone is out of line or not united in purpose and mindset. When there is a divide in this, then there can be drastic consequences to an individual or in this case to a group of people. That is why when there is leadership that is connected to God, the result is the revealing of the hidden thing, or in this case the foreign agents. Thus, this gave clarity to Joshua as to why they lost the battle. Is disunity the garment we are hiding that is causing us to lose and not see the glory of the Lord as we should?

Disunity among leadership and saints has certainly caused a great hindrance in the manifestation of God's power, thus causing defeat. Like Joshua, the battle they were instructed to engage in was met with sure defeat. Why? There was a breach within the camp. This is the case within the church body, and as a result, people are being affected. By virtue of the positions these persons hold within the church, the disease does not — dare I say cannot — remain limited to those operating in leadership capacities. These leaders cannot be quarantined in the hope of keeping the disease confined to a specific area because this disease is extremely contagious.

Thus, sadly, the disease has spread and is threatening to render the entire body of Christ powerless. It is often said, "In unity there is strength." If this saying is true, the reverse, therefore, must be true as well: "In division there is weakness and even powerlessness." The *divide and conquer* method used by the devil in these days is as old as time. Unfortunately, we seem not to have learned the lessons of the past and have allowed the devil to have his subtle but evil way among us. It's the Garden of Eden all over again — except this time, Satan is saying, "Ye shall not *surely* be strong if you are unified!"

Our leaders and even some of our parishioners are eating the fruit of division with the hope of grandeur, fame, and riches while reaping egotistical pride and self-righteousness. Consequently, the members who really want to see a manifestation of God are left to fend for themselves and, in their frustration, are scattered in search of unity. The enemy has tempted us into thinking that independence, lack of accountability, and self-motivated programs are the way to go. We cannot allow this disease to spread any further. We must pray that God would *make us one as He is one*!

From Top to Bottom

Behold, how good and how pleasant it is for brethren to dwell together in unity! It is like the precious
ointment upon the head, that ran down upon the
beard even Aaron's beard: that went down to the
skirts of his garments …

—Psalm 133:1–2

Literally, the ointment referred to in verse two is the oil of
anointing that was used by the priests in the Old Testament
to anoint a vessel or person chosen by God for His purpose.
It stands to reason, therefore, that there is a level of anointing
that cannot, and will not, be manifested in the church until
there is unity. This is a big issue. For some they will contend
that their organizational distinction allows unity completely.

The challenge to the church is not faced by naturalism of Israel or any single nation. The church is arguably fragmented
by organizationalism. We have started to mimic the systems
of the world with hopes that it will bring unity. But our carnal perspectives have thwarted our understanding that the
Kingdom of God or the body of Christ cannot be ruled or subjected to human processes and structures. Yes, organizations
and structural systems have their place, but they have to be
approached from God's perspective. Otherwise we will fall
into the same snare as Israel, which we will discuss further in
the upcoming chapter.

The direction of the flow of the ointment is symbolic of the
direction of the flow that unity must take from the top to the
bottom if it is to last and if it is to be "good and pleasant"
in the eyes and nostrils of a holy God. Since such precious
ointment flows from top to bottom, one may deduce that our
leaders are largely responsible for the discord that presently

permeates the body of Christ in many instances. Just as unity begins at the top and flows downward, so disunity begins at the top and flows downward. Using another analogy, if the top of the stream is clean, clean water will flow downstream.

How abnormal it would appear if all the lay members of the church were absolutely loving and caring even while there was constant fighting and bickering among the clergy! It is a natural law: antagonistic "parents" beget antagonistic "children" just as the anointing of the leaders flows down to their members.

The Source

> From whence come wars and fightings among you?
> Come, they not hence, even of your lusts that war
> in your members?
>
> —James 4:1

It is noteworthy that James was writing to the church, and the questions are still relevant today. James went on to rebuke the church because of her lusts. In *The Promise*, a contemporary English version of the Bible, James 4:2–3 are transliterated in this way:

> You want something you don't have and you will do anything to get it. You will even kill! But you still cannot get what you want and you won't get it by fighting and arguing. You should pray for it. Yet even when you do pray, your prayers are not answered, because you pray just for selfish reasons.

The church and more specifically those who function in leadership have forgotten that God is the source. Too many times God has been reduced to a resource to be exploited for our fleshly agendas. We have mishandled God for so long that we have reduced Him to a mere deity that responds to our every wish. Put differently, the secular construct of Santa Claus or even a genie has clouded our rightful view of God. Therefore, there must be renewed perspective of God, His precepts, and His doings.

The definition of source is useful here to bring us to consciousness and alignment to our stance of God. Webster's dictionary defines it as, "[1] the beginning: the place where something begins, where it springs into being. [2] The point of origin. [3] One that creates, causes, or initiates and or a maker" (www.websterdictionary.com). In light of this fact we have misappropriated the place where God should sit, we have witnessed the sad decline of God's presence. But when God is seated in the rightful place of Lord of lords and King of kings, we will see His majesty. We must concede that We are not lord over God's church or His people. When we acknowledge this, we will see a divine shift.

When leaders begin to make decisions out of selfish ambition rather than for the benefit of their flock, their congregation(s) will suffer. When it is more about who has the grandest church edifice or the most members rather than the propagation of the Kingdom of God, a competitive spirit, which is not of God, will thrive. When leaders start recruiting members based solely on their talent, social standing, or resourcefulness rather than on the potential each person has to become a son of God, Satan is ready to laugh gleefully.

Like Lucifer, however, anyone who seeks to shift his or her focus from God-centeredness to self-centeredness will be brought down. We must never forget that ultimately the Church is God's! That is why Jesus declared cogently, "Upon this rock I will build my church…" (Matthew 16:18). It seems that the issues on which leaders are divided are, in many cases, trivial when examined in the light of God's Word. In other words, these issues tend to have nothing to do with fundamental doctrine. While there is an agreement on the formula for salvation as established in the word of God, there are variances as it pertains certain rules. For example, Acts 2:38 portrays where the church was in a disagreement and the address that was made in light of it. Today, leaders may disagree on what kind of shoes women should be allowed to wear, whether it be open-toed, sling back, or full shoes. As a result of failing to reach a consensus, a split may ensue among the congregation over this trivial issue. And voila, a new church is born while leaders are at loggerheads!

For the most part, pastors who are not *sent* (that is, anointed and appointed by God for the purpose of leadership) but rather are created out of such divisions invariably end up becoming victims of further divisions like the ones that created them. As the saying goes, "Power corrupts; absolute power corrupts absolutely." Power is like a highly addictive drug. Man's quest for power is, as James eloquently said, the cause of the *wars and fighting* among us. The solution is a change of perception: again, we must call to mind the fact that the church is God's and that absolute power belongs to God!

Ceasefire—End the Conflict

There are countless stories of armed forces personnel who lost comrades to friendly fire. In the heat of the conflict, the same side shot, wounded, and sometimes killed their own soldiers. Cases of the sort are termed casualties of war. There are a number of reasons that cause these casualties within the church. Some arguably are trivial in nature. But there are other cases, such as disputation and fighting within the church, that have caused injury and even spiritual death to either the laity or the leadership. Somehow, though, in the heat of the battle, our vision and spiritual perspective have been blurred, and we have shot each other, in some cases unintentionally and even intentionally. The devil has amplified the heat of the battle to the extent that we have shot our allies rather than our enemies. If the devil can keep us at odds with each other, he can gain ground and affect the progression of the believer. We must remember that our enemy is the devil, not our brother or sister. Yes, there will be bouts where we will disagree with each other, but that should never lead to division.

*****

If we intend to see a mighty move of God that we say we crave in this time, then we must be prepared to follow the example of the brethren as they experienced the birth of the church in Acts 2:1: "And when the day of Pentecost was fully come they were all with one accord in one place." It is not enough for us to get together at church events and sit beside each other physically — that being the extent to which "one accord" goes. It is far beyond that. There have been too many instances where we have been in one place but not in one accord. Being in one accord means having one common expectation: to see God work, not to see flesh on parade, as is too often the case today.

Unity really works! Consider the power that emanated from a group of people of whom it was recorded: "All that believed were together and had all things common" (Acts 2:44). It can be applied today. Other secular and religious groups have discovered the power of unity. If we the church decide to share and develop the resources that exist among us — the most valuable of which is people — the entire body could benefit economically, socially, academically, physically, and above all, spiritually. Miraculous things are bound to happen when we are *in one accord*. It starts, however, with our leaders. Thus, we beseech you, leaders, lead the way into our strength!

Chapter Five

Is the Church Powerless?

And these signs shall follow them *that believe*, In my name shall they cast out devils; they shall speak with new tongues; they shall take up serpents; and if they drink any deadly thing it shall not hurt them; they shall lay hands on the sick and they shall recover.

—Mark 16:17–18

Have you stopped to consider to yourself where the power of the Acts church is?

Signs and wonders constituted a fundamental characteristic of the early church. It is noteworthy that after each miracle was wrought through the apostles as recorded in the book of the Acts, there was a significant increase of believers added to the church. Based on that fact, we too have received the power through the infilling of the Holy Spirit. Therefore, signs and wonders are an inherent part of who we are and are as relevant today as in the early church

The book of Ephesians brings clarity and context to this inheritance. This book has been considered by some as one of the most didactic of the Pauline writings. This book presents God's eternal purpose and design for the church. Paul writes about Christ as the head of the body, the church as the building, and the body as the temple of God. He goes further to explain the mystery of Christ and spiritual gifts, to list a few. But arguably, there is no other book within the New Testament that from beginning to end stimulates and revivifies one's belief in God.

In the opening verses to this prolific book, Paul is desirous that the believer would move beyond the foundational truths. He prayed that "The eyes of your understanding being enlightened…" (Ephesians 1:18).

Paul was giving the believer a combination by which to unlock the miraculous. In essence, his prayer was that the light of God's presence would flood into the inner man, thus giving revelation and illumination of our position and ultimately our inheritance in Christ Jesus — power to us who believe. Paul goes on further and exhorts the brethren to unearth what "…the hope of His calling…" This involves everything about salvation because it displays all of the great things that God has done. Hope then becomes a word of great significance. Hope, as we know, always speaks of earnest expectation. The apostle Paul was trying to convey that hope has to be the condition or state of being. Because Paul believed earnestly that receiving Jesus Christ was more than just an end in and of itself. We were created to reflect the manifestation and the power of God in the earth!

Power and Authority

Before we move forward, though, it must be established that there is a distinct difference, between power and authority. In so doing, it will provide the basis to unlock the truths and principles of the authority and power that God has invested in us. Power is the strength or force needed to rule, whereas authority is the right to carry out a specific action or duty. Authority without the power to enforce it is meaningless, and power without authority or right to use that power is usurpation and is morally wrong (Sheets 2006).

Authority, then, is delegated power. It is the value contingent upon the force behind the user. Authority is the portion of every believer. It is not something that is allotted to persons who are avid in fasting and prayer. It is an inheritance and a right to every child of God. But fasting and prayer are vital to the activation of this authority and power. Mark 9:29 stresses it this way: "And he said unto them, This kind can come forth by nothing, but by prayer and fasting."

Authority is the concept of rightful power. It is used in the Bible with a great deal of elasticity. Although the English term itself is not used in the Old Testament as in the New Testament, it is generally packaged as the word *exousia*. But the assumption permeating from both testaments is that God alone is the ultimate authority and the sole source of authority for us.

The Promise of Power ... Use It!

And, behold, I send the promise of my Father upon you: but tarry ye in the city of Jerusalem, until *ye be endued with power from on high.*

—Luke 24:49

But ye shall **receive power**, after that the Holy Ghost is come upon you: and ye shall be witnesses unto me both in Jerusalem, and in all Judaea, and in Samaria, and unto the uttermost part of the earth.

—Acts 1:8

Jesus, before His ascent back into glory, promised His disciples that power would be entrusted to them from on high. Jesus told His disciples to wait in Jerusalem until the transference of power comes. Jesus then emphasized its source and commissioned them to do greater works than He did (John 14:12). When the disciples received this promise, the book of Acts shows how they manifested the power of God. It was the unrestricted flow of the power of Jehovah! It was a power that was not derived by natural means but was and is purely supernatural. As such, it could not be constrained by natural forces.

Thus, the believer must grab hold of the fullness of this promise. At some point or another in the church experience, the Holy Ghost has been reduced to simply speaking in tongues. But speaking in tongues is just the identification of the residing power of God in one's life. A fair assessment is that, if God is in us, we have power—a power that was not intended to be capped or restrained but rather to be used for the glorification of God.

The poignant question that needs to be asked is whether the Holy Ghost was just given simply for self-gratification and pleasure. Or is it a sensation that we experience and encounter in the confines of church?

The Power to Us-Ward Who Believe!

And what is the exceeding greatness of his power to us-ward who believe, according to the working of his mighty power.

—Ephesians 1:19

To get the fullness of this verse and the meanings of *authority* and *power,* this verse needs to be viewed in a partial transliterated form in order to glean the interwoven truths.

> The exceeding greatness of his [God's] power [*dunameos*] to us-ward who believe, according to the working [*Energeion*] of the strength [*Kratous*] of his might.

To believe is a fundamental component for one to see and be a recipient of the working of God's strength and might. That is why there is such emphasis throughout the New Testament writings to ingrain it into the mind and spirit of the reader. Now the word *power* in this verse is of much importance as well.

The word *power* comes from the Greek word *dunamis,* from which we get two words. It is from here that we get the word dynamite. Dunamis means, "The ability to accomplish something." Paul was simply saying that it is God's power, and He is the only one who can accomplish or handle the impossible. The application that must be made here is that we have to learn to appropriate this concept to our Christian living.

The other word for dunamis is also of importance. It is *dynamo.* There is a stark difference in dynamite and dynamo. A dynamo is not explosive or as noisy. Rather, it is a continuous power. It is constantly there, and it will not end (Barber, 2011). It is clear what the unique properties of dynamite are, but dynamo reinforces the consistency of this word, which means "power to accomplish something." In other words, it is an unrelenting power that will not cease to accomplish. Do we realize that there is a surpassing greatness of His power to us?

Authority—It's Your Inheritance, So Use It!

You can only have authority when you are under authority. The Bible tells us that God has "... made us sit together in heavenly places in Christ Jesus:" (Ephesians 2:6).

The word *sit* here is symbolic of the word authority or the place of rulership. This position or posture in which one can make rulings is simply because of the redemptive work of the cross. We are inheritors of this promise and thus have the right to exercise our God-given ability. But the enemy has placed strategic interferences, such as disbelief, to disable us in operating at the frequency and might that we should have. Mark 5:6 brings to light that not even Jesus could do any great works because of disbelief. Too many times disbelief has aborted the workings of God in our churches. Thus, disbelief negates the power and workings of God.

The byword that is used frequently throughout the book of Ephesians is belief, which is beneficial to unlock the manifestation of God. The latter clause of Ephesians 1:19 is paramount in coming to grips with what God has bestowed to us. But there is a condition that must be followed: "...to us-ward who *believe*..."

The word belief has a twofold meaning that has deep significance. The word believe means "to live or exist." Thus, to believe literally means "to live in accordance with anything that God has prescribed through his word." The concept we have embraced for belief has been deduced to simply a mental agreement with a particular truth. But it needs to be highlighted that the root meaning of this word leads one to action. In other words, belief then can be synonymous with faith. Faith then will prompt movement and create evidence.

But with prosperity on the rise and the increase in the advancements of technology and science, the twenty-first-century church's level of faith has waned, and the output of God limited. At one point, faithlessness could be ascribed only to the secular world, but now it has filtered into the very fabric and mindset of the church. As a result, there are many perplexed people in the pews day after day and night after night who seem to feel that there is no sense in believing, particularly when they perceive that nothing is going to happen. They have opted to be content with the state or condition that they are in.

Similarly, the lame man at the gate beautiful in Acts 3 had the same outlook. He was sitting at the temple gate at the hour of prayer begging for alms. It is important to note the place and time in which Scripture records this occurrence. It was at the temple during the time of prayer. In other words, there is something that needs to be said about time and place. But Peter, by divine authority, offered him something of great worth. Peter declared, demonstrating *dunamis* and *dynamo*: "...Silver and gold have I none; but such as I have give I thee: In the name of Jesus Christ of Nazareth rise up and walk."

This state of stepping out on divine authority and power resulted in the following:

> And he took him by the right hand, and lifted him
> Up: and immediately his feet and ankle bones received strength. And he leaping up stood, and
> walked, and entered with them into the temple,
> walking, and leaping and praising God.
>
> — Acts 3:7–8

Scripture highlights how this act of authority altered the ninth hour of prayer. When the miraculous begins to happen, it will affect the set church program. It will arrest the spirit of mediocrity and challenge unbelief.

When you are under divine authority of Jehovah, you are able to speak the word or perform a certain task, and there is a manifestation of the working of God. But this can only occur when people have truly subjected themselves to the sovereign rule of Jehovah.

Demonstrate the Power!

I felt that it was necessary to include some testimonies of miraculous workings of God to strengthen our faith. Too many times miracles have been attributed to things of the past or obsolete or random occurrences. But each of these testimonies are just reminders that God remains faithful and tied to His Word.

Boy in Car Accident—Healed

God remains constant and cannot change. The power of the Acts is still very much active. There have been great moves of God I have witnessed while ministering in various parts of the world. In the spring of 2007, I was ministering in Jamaica, West Indies, and a member of that particular church was informed that her stepson was accidently hit by a car at school. He was taken to a nearby hospital, where he was admitted for injuries to his shoulder and hip. Upon examination by the doctors, it was concluded that it would take a few months for this boy to walk again. At the height of the service, I was informed about this boy's condition and was requested to pray for him, which I did. But after praying for him, I was impressed by the Lord to give his stepmother a blessed handkerchief. I told her to place it on his hip and shoulder when she went back to the hospital. As instructed, the next day the stepmother went to the hospital and placed the handkerchief on her stepson's injuries. On the following day, the stepmother received a telephone call from the hospital informing her that her stepson had been discharged and needed to be picked up because he had been miraculously healed and was now able to walk.

Reversal to Baby in a Breech Position

In May of 2007, I visited another church in Jamaica. A young lady who attended this church was in her final stage of pregnancy and her baby was in a breech position. She came up to the front during altar call and requested prayer. The host pastor invited me to the front to pray with this young lady. Before doing so, the young lady told me what the problem was regarding her pregnancy. As I was impressed by the Spirit of the Lord, I asked one of the ladies to anoint her belly. We prayed and earnestly believed that God would change the position of this baby. We spoke with apostolic authority to this baby in womb. A few days later, I received a phone call that the baby was born in a normal position and that the baby was all right.

From Barrenness to Bearing a Child

In 2008, I was ministering at a conference in New Jersey and a couple who were members of this church had been married for ten years and were desperately trying to have a child. The doctors told them that they would not be able to conceive any children in their lifetime. Despite the heart-wrenching diagnosis of the doctor, this couple tried to uphold their faith and trust in God. The couple expressed to me that they contemplated going to the conference the night that I was ministering. But the husband felt compelled that they both should attend.

In the conclusion of my message that night, I felt the strong thrust of God to pray for this couple. I declared by apostolic authority and power to the congregation that in six weeks they would conceive a child. Now this couple has a beautiful baby boy. But what adds to this miracle is that the wife was forty-four years old when she gave birth to her baby.

These testimonies dispel the notion that the miracles of the Bible are just fables. God still does the extraordinary, and we have to believe and accept that His Word must accomplish what it sets out to do. God's Word is active and living!

He Is Still the God of Then and Now!

Without a doubt, God still remains the same. Albert Einstein put it best when he said, "God is the unmoved mover." Regardless of the advancements of science and technology, the power of God is still constant and inherent in the church. There will be a people now who will no longer accept being slaves to illness and the diagnoses of doctors but will tap into the inheritance to us who believe. Even though this twenty-first-century generation brags about the success of their accomplishments in science and technology, it has not minimized the power and authority. Unfortunately, it has caused so many of us to lose faith in the supernatural and put confidence in the natural.

There is much we can learn from natural power that can give us insight to the spiritual condition happening within the church. If you examine energy specifically, you will find two categories of energy: potential and kinetic. Potential energy is simply untapped energy-in-waiting that is yet to be deployed — for example, the chemicals in a battery or a stretched rubber band. Kinetic energy is energy in full motion, such as a car in full acceleration speeding down the roadway. Clearly, energy can change form. Similarly, we have this innate ability by the spirit of God to move. Jesus, before ascending up into heaven, sat with His disciples. He commissioned them and promised them:

> And these signs shall follow them that believe; In my name shall they cast out devils; they shall speak with new tongues; They shall take up serpents; and if they drink any deadly thing, it shall not hurt them; they shall lay hands on the sick, and they shall recover.
>
> — Mark 16:17–18

The death, burial, and resurrection of Jesus changed the balance of power. At the brink of Jesus's ascension, the rights to the release of power were conferred to the believer. The name of Jesus is the access code for the demonstration of this power. A power that Jesus declared would be a sign that would follow the believer. This power cannot simply remain in a potential form in the believer but must be converted into kinetic power. In other words, it is time for activation, demonstration, and manifestation of the power of God. God did not dispense this power for it to be contained for our personal benefit alone. Rather, it has to be released as a sign of the power of God.

Chapter Six

The Church—a God Thought!

To the intent that now unto the principalities and powers in heavenly places might be known by the church the manifold wisdom of God. According to the eternal purpose which he purposed in Christ Jesus our Lord.

—Ephesians 3:10–11

The church is a glorious and divine entity created to reveal the mysteries of Jesus Christ. It transcends the impact of globalization, the power of corporate giants on Wall Street, and even the complexities of relativism and quantum physics, to name a few. The church cannot be affected by the rise and fall of governments, the economy, and the environment. It is an entity that is beyond the confines of natural laws and the comprehension of mankind.

As a matter of fact, it is a living organism that cannot be crippled or rendered powerless due to the human stressors of labor, inflation, capital, recession, etc. The church is a God idea that is at the center of God's heart and thought. It has been and is an integral part of His purpose since the beginning of time.

The Purpose and Design of the Church

A thorough understanding of the definition, purpose, and design of the church is vital for us to present it effectively to the world. In the New Testament writings, the Greek word for church is *ekklesia,* meaning "a gathering of those called." The other Greek word that is frequently used is *kuriakon,* which denotes a place. It is believed that it is from that word the English word *church* has its derivative. But regardless of man's definitions, God's perspective and definition of the church is solely about His people.

In his letter to the Ephesians, Paul expounds a clear indication as to the church's mandate. This mandate can be viewed as being twofold:

1. To perfect and edify the body of Christ

2. To make disciples of men

As such, the church should be a place where love and compassion are manifestly practiced. It should also be a place where one can come to the consciousness of one's true design as set out in Scriptures, irrespective of ethnicity, gender, or creed.

Paul goes on further to express that God's design for the church is to gather all creation under the Lordship of Christ (Ephesians 1:10), thus bringing humanity into communion with Him. As a reflection of this, the church is to manifest God's mercy and compassion to humankind. By so doing, humanity will be restored to their original purpose, which is to glorify God in concurrence with the heavenly host. The intent of God, then, is that through the church, humanity will be drawn to the goal of restoration and salvation. The apex of this divine plan is the elevation of man to his rightful place of communion with God, resulting in eternal bliss with Him in a new heaven and earth (Revelation 21:1).

What the Church Is *Not*

There are countless sermons, lectures, books, articles, and many other resources that provide information about what the church is. But rarely do we uncover what the church is not. In Mark Connor's book, *Transforming Your Church*, he captures it succinctly by putting it this way:

The Church is *not* a building

The Church is *not* an organization

The Church is *not* one particular nationalistic group.

Reinforcing what the church is not provides greater clarity as to its true purpose and design. So many times our conception of the church has been synonymous with a building rather than embracing it as a spiritual entity. In so doing, we have unintentionally minimized the power that is truly inherent in the church. The book of Acts clearly shows the church in action. The action was not confined to a particular location, yet God manifested Himself through miraculous deeds! Thus, when the church experience can only be derived from within a sanctuary, it will sidetrack the intended purpose and power of God.

Sadly, this outlook has permeated Christendom, so most spiritual activities and experiences with God have been confined within the four walls of a building. This parochial stance has thwarted our purpose as believers. In Matthew 28:19–20, the commission of the church is clearly stated to the entire unit or grouping of believers. It declares:

> Go ye therefore, and teach all nations, baptizing
> them in the *name* of the Father, and of the Son, and
> of the Holy Ghost: Teaching them to observe all
> things whatsoever I have commanded you: and,
> lo, I am with you alway, even unto the end of the
> world. Amen.

When there is a renewed commitment to follow the commission of the church, it will ignite a powerful move of God in the earth. But when we willingly negate this as our responsibility, we dwarf the output that God has for us. In so doing, the church cannot operate or function at the intensity and with the strength that God purposed. Consequently, we have employed natural or corporate structures, formulas, and ideas, seeking to get spiritual results. Man-made and man-run ideas are weak and powerless to heal a decaying world. There is certainly no contention that Christendom has the form—a building—but the resounding question is, where is the power of God necessary to make a difference in a disintegrating world?

The Gates of Hell Shall Not Prevail

> And I say unto thee, That thou art Peter, and upon
> this rock I will build my church; and the gates of
> hell shall not prevail against it.
>
> —Matthew 16:18

Jesus, the apostle Paul, and others in the New Testament gave us a glimpse of the future and made heartfelt pleas to the church to watch for wolves in sheep's clothing. These forefathers' insights into this time period are being manifested on a grand scale. We are witnessing some of the greatest levels of apostasy, spiritual decline, and humanism the church has ever seen.

Today the church is being viewed and treated as a business venture. Seemingly, it has become the new enterprise that needs updating and revisions. The modern church believes the outlined tenets of the faith are no longer relevant and as such need to be revitalized. These reformers have defended these actions by simply asserting, "We are not changing the content; we are just changing the package." All of this is designed to attract the masses and at the same time, generate revenue. But no where in these new formulations is there any mention or consideration of God's requirements and His design and purpose for the church. Inadvertently, these reformers have enunciated that God's design of the church cannot retain its intensity or value over time. In other words, these repackaging agents in Christendom are simply conveying that the church depreciates with time or with sociopolitical pressures of the day.

Clearly, this revival to reform the church has been disseminated at an alarming rate, to the extent that leadership and its congregations are abandoning the fundamentals of the true church. They embrace this new paradigm, ostensibly to get results—meaning large congregations, the creation of programs. The outlook is, if the church does not possess these qualities (large congregations and cutting-edge programs), it is not productive or growing. Oddly, we have been led to believe that we can assess God's church from our finite minds. But the apostle Paul gives a solemn indictment and points out, "...the carnal mind is enmity against God" (Romans 8:7). The word *carnal* here signifies fleshy. That is to say that it is natural. How can a carnal mind that is against God perceive or even understand a spiritual organism? How can it be relegated to humanistic confines and then be identified as the church?

One will notice that in Acts 20, Paul mentions nothing about marketing, growing, or adapting. Instead he warns the church to teach the whole counsel of God — to beware of false teachers and to preach the gospel of faith and repentance, which has stirred up a major debate within the church growth movement. It can be described as "watering down" the gospel message. But before we can move any further, it needs to be asserted that when God began to move within the Acts church, the signs and wonders became marketing tools. Put differently, when God moves, people will come.

Being politically correct has become a societal norm that is altering the manner in which we address and deal with each other. It has become something of great debate and sensitivity. Today we are solicited to be sensitive so as not to offend or exclude anyone. This societal norm has influenced the content of the gospel message. The message of repentance has become something to be tailored so as not to make one feel out of place or guilty. But the gospel is not about making one feel better about oneself. Rather, it is to bring people to the consciousness that they are guilty, lost, and perishing.

This attempt to appeal to masses has meant that the message that exposes sin by condemning it cannot be politically correct and subsequently not marketable. Yet this new gospel is being presented as an attractive item to the sinner that liberates, boosts self-esteem, fills personal emptiness, and provides a sense of excitement and a pseudo sense of spiritual awakening. Although some of this falls in line with what salvation brings, the fundamentals are being omitted, thus rendering the church powerless and unidentifiable to the world.

Acts 5:11–13 discloses that the manifestation of God in the church at Jerusalem caused many to fear God and even to join its ranks. The book of Acts also highlights that the preaching of Paul had a fiery conviction. Acts 20:20 states that Paul "kept back nothing," reproving, rebuking, and exhorting with all longsuffering and bearing in mind a future time when people would no longer

> endure sound doctrine, but according to their own desires, because they have itching ears, they will heap up for themselves teachers and they will turn their ears away from the truth.
>
> 2 Timothy 4:2–4

That day has surely come—a gospel that no longer has a classification such as saints but rather customers who take priority over God. This new paradigm has in many cases subverted the true gospel message, and as such, exposition has been swapped for entertainment, preaching for performance, doctrine for drama, and theology for theatrics—and the fallout has been catastrophic (Penfold 2011).

Despite the cunning works of the enemy, the gates of hell will not and cannot prevail. The church is not built on the whims or concepts of a man. The church is a God-designed, God-led, God-centered, and God-focused institution. While the local church (assembly) might be characterized as ruled and directed by a specific man, the church (mystic) is a divine entity that cannot be constrained by the devices of autocracy or democracy. The church is a divine plan that came out of the heart of God. And God will have a church that is glorious and spotless from the world.

Chapter Seven

Faith Will Find a Way

Great faith is the product of great fights
Great testimonies are the outcome of great tests
Great triumphs can only come out of great trials

—Smith Wigglesworth

And Jesus said unto them, Because of your unbelief:
for verily I say unto you, If ye have faith as a grain
of mustard seed, ye shall say unto this mountain,
Remove hence to yonder place; and it shall remove;
and nothing shall be impossible unto you.

—Matthew 17:20

Faith is a word that is often waved or thrown around in Christendom with no real thought of its meaning and importance. Many times, faith has simply been reduced to belief, when in fact the Scripture speaks at length about this biblical concept. One preacher uniquely defined faith as, "Forsaking All, I Trust Him." The apostle Paul gives us a starting point to understand faith in 2 Corinthians 5:7: "For we walk by faith, not by sight." Then he adds to it by saying, "Faith cometh by hearing and hearing by the word of God." Romans 10:17

Each of Paul's definitions implies some type of action. However, *Webster's New World Dictionary* defines faith as, "complete trust, confidence, reliance and belief." One will note that at the end of this definition, belief is listed as a synonym of faith. Belief means, "Faith, especially religious faith; as trust or confidence" (www.thefreedictionary.com). These dictionary definitions clearly show that these two words are virtually synonymous. But the Bible highlights, particularly through practical application, the wide differences that separate merely belief and living by faith. The practical application of faith is more than simply acknowledging or believing in God. The key to faith as highlighted in the New Testament writings is living by faith. Faith then requires an action and supersedes just a mental state. Like Peter walking on the water, faith requires one to act! Faith without works is dead. Thus, the aim of this chapter is to revisit this foundational biblical concept and encourage the believer to step out on faith. Sadly, our scientific and technology age has influenced our perspectives, and our faith has waned as result. So many of us have concluded that faith and faith works, for that matter, are things of the past and only rational and informed actions must happen today.

When Your Faith Is Challenged

In Norman Lamm's book, *Faith and Doubt: Studies in Traditional Jewish Thoughts,* he presents faith in a unique way. He states,

> Faith, like life itself, is paradoxically both weak and strong. It is delicate, and sometimes falls apart at the slightest infection with doubt. At the same time, it is remarkable, resilient, tenacious, and tough: it somehow manages to survive the heaviest onslaughts. Wounded, bruised, even humiliated,

it often recuperates and regains its wholeness, its
health, and its dignity.

Norman Lamm's view on faith dispels the misconceptions
that faith is not without pain and process. Hebrews 11 provides a catalog of people who have demonstrated over-
coming faith—faith that survived in the crucible of existence;
faith that flourished under fire; faith that knew how to hold
on and hold out. Hebrews 11 calls to mind such notables as
Abel, Noah, and Abraham. As seen throughout Scripture,
the pages are filled with poignant men and women of God
who stepped out in unwavering faith and saw mighty acts of
God. Men and women like Enoch, Noah, Abraham, Rahab,
Barak, and many others have names that are etched in the
hallmark of faith. Their fervor and devotion even in the face
of adversity and challenge is what is noteworthy to consider.
It is easy, though, to focus on their victories and quickly gloss
over the painstaking stance that was required. What was it
that kept them so confident and reliant upon God even when
confronted with disappointment and death? Did the obstacles
or hardships they encountered only strengthen their resolution and conviction?

Hebrews 11:13 denotes to us the internal working of God of
these champions of faith: "These all died in faith, not having received the promises, but having seen them afar off, and
were persuaded of them, and embraced them, and confessed
that they were strangers and pilgrims on the earth." This hall
of champions prompted the following question: what do you
do when you have acted in faith but the outcome was the opposite of what you expected? As a result, your faith is challenged as to whether to believe God or to succumb to pressure and chaos of your circumstance. James 1:3–4 says, "The
testing of your faith produces patience. But let patience have

its perfect work, that you may be perfect and complete, lacking nothing."

Our faith, as precious as it is, must be tested. It must be tried to be matured and perfected. That is why it is imperative that we respond in the right way to foster a personal stance that encourages and strengthens our faith even when confronted with hardship, disappointment, and loss.

It should be noted that your faith can grow, and it can also wane or decrease. This can occur when you are confronted with adversity and challenges. These vicissitudes may oftentimes feel like you have been hit by a two-by-four. As a result, your faith level may drop. It is at that point that you must determine within yourself to return to a place of faith in God. For example, when a professional athletic team is losing a game, the coach will generally give them a pep talk to get them out of the slump.

As this concept is true in the natural, so it is in the supernatural. From time to time, you will have to give yourself a pep talk to maintain your faith levels from waning when adversity hits. You have to declare the promises of God in the midst of the hardships and difficulties. Yes, it can and will be arduous at times, but remain focused on the promise keeper! God will not put more on you than you are able to bear. First Corinthians 10:13 expresses it this way:

> There hath no temptation taken you but such as is common to man: but God is faithful, who will not suffer you to be tempted above that ye are able; but will with the temptation also make a way to escape, that ye may be able to bear it.

In the Greek, the word "temptation" here translates to testing and trials. The apostle Paul reminds us that tests and trials are an experience that no one is exempt from. It is a common human condition, but God remains faithful and provides a provision in the midst of it. The consolation rooted in this verse is that God is ever present—even in the immediacy of your test. That is why you cannot give up, because in due season God will eventually deliver you.

The account of Moses and the children of Israel in the wilderness is a perfect example. Due to the older Israelites' unbelief and failure to adhere to the word of God, they could not enter the Promised Land. Their faith was inoperative, and as a result, they were unfit to lay claim to the Promised Land and what it included. This account is important for us to observe in that if we fail to maintain a healthy faith level, it may prohibit us from receiving the promises of God.

The Bible outlines that only Joshua, Caleb, and the younger generation could enter. The prolonged journey and hardships of the wilderness did not erode Joshua or Caleb's faith. When they were confronted with this painstaking task of taking the Promised Land, they did not waver but rather maintained their faith in the Lord. Their faith gave them the fortitude to combat against the giants in the land. The wilderness became the place where God proved them. Our wilderness is pivotal in determining whether we can posses the promise. This account shows us that Joshua was victorious and that he acquired every square meter of the land his foot had stepped on, all because his faith and belief in God were strong.

There are contemporary examples that are beneficial for us to explore. Recently I had the opportunity to talk with a young lady at a church where I was ministering. She expressed to me that her faith was challenged to a point that she had never experienced before. She informed me that she had received the most shocking news that her full-time job was going to be eliminated due to restructuring within the organization. She told me that the news felt as though a fierce and sudden wind had just blown. The feeling was daunting and overwhelming. Yet in the midst of this, she affirmed that God intervened and reminded her that He had heard her earlier prayers to be removed from this painful and stressful work environment.

She went on further to relay that God sent peace to her mind and emotions. While driving home, she welled up with tears because of the shock of this news. In the midst of this, she received an encouraging text message stating, "All hope is not lost." Immediately she felt a strong presence of the Lord and relief.

She stated that she continued to seek the Lord consistently for clarity and direction. She expressed that Romans 8:28 was vital in maintaining her faith in all of this uncertainty. As a result, she began to search for a new job and the enemy began to plague her mind with discouragement and frustration. But in all this, her confidence in God grew. Finally, she stated that God led her to a job posting that was much higher than her previous job. In faith, she submitted her application to prove God.

She articulated to me that two days before her interview, God gave her a song of consolation. She said that she knew this interview would be extraordinary. The moment she met the interviewer, there was a divine intervention. She went on to say that the atmosphere was very calm and peaceful. The interviewer indicated after the interview that a response would be given within a week. She said that in two days, she was offered the position from a pool of sixty-five candidates. She also alluded to the fact that the job was a higher level and pay with a peaceful work atmosphere. This situation confirms that even in the present we can maintain our faith even when we are confronted with unexpected testing's. God still remains mindful and faithful to His promises. Psalm 138:8 tells us, "The Lord will perfect that which concerneth me: Thy loving kindness, O Jehovah, endureth for ever; Forsake not the works of thine own hands."

God will complete what He has begun. This verse states that God will. It does not say maybe but that it is an absolute fact. Therefore, God will not initiate contact with us and then abandon us. He will not instruct us to have faith and not honor it. He will not allow us to go through fiery trials and leave us to fend for ourselves. God will complete what He begins. But we must first have faith in the personage and promises of God!

Doubt—a Diabolical Opponent to Faith

In the synoptic gospels, Jesus spoke about the insidious power of disbelief. Jesus highlighted through parables how doubt could hinder the very workings of God. Webster's definition of doubt is needful for the believer to grasp the nature of this spirit. It is defined as, "to waver in opinion; fearful, apprehensive or suspicious of" (www.yourdictionary.com). Today, this spirit has masked itself in fact—something that can be substantiated or proved, which oftentimes is more readily accepted than faith. Romans 14:23 tells us, "Whatever is not of faith is sin." One can deduce that whatever is of faith is pleasing before God. Faithlessness can no longer be something that is an acceptable posture for the Christian. We must have faith to please God; otherwise it is sin. Too many times we have placed a ranking system to sin, and generally faithlessness is not included in that ranking.

Hebrews 11:1 in the Amplified Bible captures the true characteristics of faith this way:

> Now faith is the [substance] assurance (the con-
> firmation, the title deed) of the things [we] hope
> for, being the proof of things [we] do not see and
> the conviction of their reality [faith perceiving as
> real fact what is not revealed to the senses].

In this verse Paul uniquely uses the words "substance" and
"evidence," which generally speaks of something tangible
or natural. That is a why a quick glimpse at the meanings of
these words will give us a greater understanding of faith. The
word substance here in the Greek is *hypostasis* which means:
"a setting under or support, foundation, assurance, and a confident expectation." Faith in relation to our hope is assurance.
It stands under and supports our hope. Thus, one's hope is
only as secure as one's faith is strong.

The word evidence here is referred to as conviction. It is defined as a "proof or proving" (www.yourdictionary.com). In
other words, faith is not a blind acceptance of improvable
opinions, guesswork, nor a feeling or emotion. It is conviction
supported by evidence, which is the infallible word of God.
Put differently, the word, that is commonly referred to as the
seed of God, is inextricably linked to faith (Luke 8:11). When it
is mixed with faith, the germination process will begin. Romans 10:17 states, "Faith cometh by hearing, and hearing by the
word of God." The prerequisite of faith is the word of God.
If we are to see the intangible of the unseen realm, we must
study the Word or the evidence. The Word is spirit ... Faith,
then, by its very nature, begins and ends in the realm of the
unseen and is not revealed to the senses. Hence, the aim is to
highlight that doubt cripples and restricts one to the natural
realm, and as a result, fear comes in and faith is dispelled!

One of the explicit teachings of the Bible refers to the importance of the words we utilize. In other words, the word of God

is designed to be applied to the life of the believer. The word is the sole basis to our faith.

Radical Faith!

The Bible clearly demarcates the radical stance of faith. Faith is not something that can be readily understood by the human intellect; as a matter of fact, faith challenges and steps outside of the confines of what is generally considered logical or normal. Put differently, faith transforms from oxymoron to provable fact. Clearly, there is no shortage of examples that are displayed throughout the entire canon of Scripture. Men and women who defied insurmountable odds thus showcased the power of God. Matthew 17:20 states:

> [If] ye have faith as a grain of mustard seed, ye shall say unto this mountain, Remove hence to yonder place; and it shall remove; and nothing shall be impossible unto you.

It is important to point out that a mustard seed is the smallest of all seeds. Jesus, with the use of this analogy, was telling His disciples that if they had even a small faith, they would command whatever they would and it would be done. Along with that, this Scripture tells us that faith does not require a large quantity, but a diminutive mustard seed will suffice to move the impossible.

Jesus Himself established the importance of understanding how faith works when He said, "...touched he their eyes, saying, According to your faith be it unto you. (Matthew 9:29). In other words, where there is no possession or action of faith, there can be no workings of God. Faith requires action on our part. We are not a neutral party, but we must observe what God outlined in His Word, and our posture and speech must conform to it. We must start to agree with God's Word. Put differently, where God has spoken on a matter, we can take His word to the bank, as the old saying goes. Second Peter 3:9 states, "The Lord is not slack concerning his promises, as some men count slackness ..." God is not tardy or slow about what He promises but will fulfill His Word. God's Word is His bond. Today, what we say many times does not coincide with what we mean, and as such, our words are meaningless or fruitless. But with God, it is completely contrary to man.

In conjunction with this, Hebrews 11:6 puts it in this light:

> But without faith it is impossible to please him: for he that cometh to God must believe that he is, and that he is a rewarder of them that diligently seek him.

The book of Habakkuk parallels this Scripture by saying that "... the just shall live by his faith." This tells us that faith is a lifestyle by which a just man lives. The word just here means approved, which speaks to one's relationship with God, which is by faith. Therefore, living by faith is not a mere momentary action but a continuous state of being. Oftentimes we live or are governed by our feelings, ideologies, circumstances, and other external influences. But God is requiring us to forsake natural perspectives and thus directs us to live by faith! Mahatma Gandhi, one of history's greatest peace activists, understood the need for and power of faith and stated, "Faith can only grow from within, it cannot be acquired vicariously. Nothing great in this world was ever accomplished without a living faith."

Gandhi's peaceful demonstration spoke to his personal resolve and faith, and he changed the course of history. Gandhi's consciousness of the need to have faith is noteworthy here and should impact us to the point that we take greater thought as to whether we are living in faithlike manner. Faith can no longer be just a biblical concept we speak about; it must become a compass to our lifestyle as a believer. Therefore, it is important for us to consider that if we are going to please God and live above sin, we must live by faith! Faith is the starting point to receive the bountiful blessings and provisions of God. Walk by faith … take the first step!

Chapter Eight

Christian Living

Going to church won't make you a Christian any more
than going to a garage will make you a mechanic.

Today there is an influx of self-help and how-to books with
the aim of getting people to evaluate their current life practices and consider the improvement tips offered to reach the
zenith of happiness that life has to offer. Oftentimes the picture that is first painted is that your current life practices will
inhibit you from experiencing happiness unless you do what
is recommended. Then suggestions are offered with a guarantee that change will happen within a specified timeframe.
If it doesn't, then the sudden conclusion is that the recipient
did not follow the set guidelines to the letter. Generally this
promise to attain a sense of happiness or pleasure is purely
subjective.

This preoccupation to improve life is not limited to beauty
tips, health, and wellness but reaches to addressing the emotional and spiritual aspects of a person. This pursuit of trying
to get people to become one with their selves and be the best
they can be has arguably spawned a large demographic of
people who have become insecure in who they are.

Proverbs is in a section of the Bible known as "Wisdom Literature." The other books in this section are Job, Psalms, Ecclesiastes, and the Song of Solomon. The focus of these books is to instruct men in the ways of the Lord and in His service and worship. The book of Proverbs is a collection of teachings from Solomon to his son, showing the young man how to live his life in a manner that is pleasing to the Lord. I would say that we all need that kind of instruction, wouldn't you?

If there is a key verse that unlocks the power and purpose of this great book, it would be the verse we have just read. If we are to learn wisdom and knowledge, it must begin with the fear of the Lord. This is a subject that isn't preached about much in our day, but it is still vital to the Christian's faith. We need to know what the fear of the Lord is all about.

This is a very vital line of thought in the book of Proverbs, as it is mentioned roughly eighteen times in its pages. In all, the phrase can be found twenty-seven times in the Bible. If so much emphasis is placed on fearing the Lord, then I believe we need to know what it means and how we can go about doing it. Therefore, I would like to elaborate from this book on the fear of the Lord. I believe the Lord wants to teach us what this matter of fearing Him is all about. He wants you and me to grow in our relationship with Him and in our knowledge of Him, and the way knowledge begins is with the fear of the Lord.

It's Beyond the Knowing of God

Not everyone that saith unto me, Lord, Lord, shall enter into the kingdom of heaven; but he that doeth the will of my Father which is in heaven. Many will say to me in that day, Lord, Lord, have we not prophesied in thy name? and in thy name have we cast out devils? and in thy name done many wonderful works? And then will I profess unto them, I never knew you: depart from me, ye that work iniquity.

—Matthew 7:21–23

Matthew, the gospel writer, clearly says that God is more interested in relationship than ministry. The word *knew* in verse 23 reinforces this. The Greek word for knew is *ginosko*, which refers to the context of "an intimate relationship, union and or approval." An alternative definition is also useful here: "to know with favor" (www.biblestudytools.com)

On one of my trips to England in early 2000, I asked a fellow minister if he could truly say he knows God—a question that had him thinking deeply and intently. His honest response to me was he had never considered the question in such a way. This simple yet profound question greatly impacted his Christian life in a positive way from then on.

The challenge of the believer is to move beyond the concept of just knowing about God to the posture of intimacy. A phrase that has been frequently used to simplistically define the word intimacy is "into me see." God wants to reveal to us the secrets of who He is and thus instructs us to undress ourselves from the garments that would impede us from becoming intimate. The fear of the Lord is one of the defining components of intimacy with God. When one possesses reverential awe and respect for God, it sets the tone for revelation, protection, providence, etc. Psalm 25:14 highlights one of the principles of intimacy: "The secret of the LORD is with them that fear him; and he will shew them his covenant."

Put differently, only when one possesses the fear of the Lord can one truly engage intimately with God. Lack of fear of the Lord means no revealing of His secrets. That is why we are commissioned to undress, so we can become open to walk with and experience the favor and approval of God.

In Zechariah 2:9, God declares that we are the apple of His eye, and as such He longs to have a close relationship with us. God desires that we spend time with Him in intimate communication and fellowship. This time spent with God ultimately gives our life meaning and purpose. Oswald Chambers expresses it this way:

> It is a joy to Jesus when a person takes time to walk more intimately with Him. The bearing of fruit is always shown in Scripture to be a visible result of an intimate relationship with Jesus.

It is absolutely impossible to have an intimate relationship with God and not have His divine attributes or qualities! The gospels carefully set out how the impact of Jesus affected the lives of His disciples, even to the extent of their speech.

Ministry vs. Relationship

There are many examples scattered throughout the canon of Scripture that showcase the manifest workings of God, many of which can cause our carnal minds to ponder or question how and why these great miracles came to pass. The way of God, as we have seen, usually supersedes every natural law, be it the laws of physics, biology, and so on, thus causing conflict with the human psyche. This is simply how God works! Yet even beyond the workings of such powerful miracles and signs as seen throughout the Scriptures, God is more interested in a relationship with His creation. Oftentimes there has been such emphasis on gifting(s), talent, and the ability to perform that the priority has shifted from having a relationship with God. Therefore, there needs to be careful consideration of some of the examples of old and how their relationship with God gave rise to the flow of the miraculous.

It has been said that couples who have been married for a while begin to look like each other after a number of years. In other words, the closeness of their relationship causes others to view them as looking alike. When one has a relationship with God, the result is similar. The manifestation of God through our lives will cause us to begin to look like God! Moses's encounter on Mount Sinai is a prime example of how one's life course and even one's physical appearance can be divinely altered by embracing a relationship with a loving God.

As a matter of fact, the ultimate plan of God for our lives is that we have a relationship with Him. Oh how God yearns that we would make Him the object of our affection. For so long we have sought after the fringe benefits of God but we have never really explored the fullness of an unlimited God through relationship. A point that needs to be underscored here is that when Adam was created by God, he was not created to preach, teach, or fulfill any other ministerial function as we know them. Rather he was created for the sole purpose of communing with God.

God created Adam simply for relationship! When His relationship with Adam was disconnected because of disobedience, sin entered into the world and humankind was separated from its Creator. As a result, God's love impelled Him to set a course within time to bring man back to his former state. The cross then became the hallmark that solemnly proclaimed the heart and the point of reference man could use to get back to God. In summation, all of the acts of God as seen throughout the Scriptures, whether miraculous healings or prophecies, were simply methods to point us to the original design of man—fellowship with the Almighty!

A relationship with God should be so endearing and captivating to us beyond mere ministry. It is an awesome privilege when we are selected to minister, but ministry operates on the realm of "for God," whereas relationship is a realm of "with God." These are two very different realms that must be considered and observed. Why do I seek God? Is it for the fishes and loaves of ministry? Or do I want God for Himself? These are questions we need to ask ourselves. A relationship with God is the most important thing in our Christian walk!

Throughout the books of the New Testament there is information about Christian living. The New Testament writers spend a considerable amount of time highlighting the characteristics and traits of being a Christian. These writers even express the challenges the believer will face. The worldly systems of the day have made it a painstaking and challenging experience to live as a Christian. Because of the intensity of the challenges coming from the world, so many Christians have opted to a have "modified" or a "part-time" Christian status. But the Pauline writer confirms and consoles us that we are more than conquerors, and as such, we have the ability, with God's help, to live a victorious Christian life.

In His Presence

> ...In thy presence is fullness of joy, at thy right hand
> there are pleasures forevermore.
>
> — Psalm 16:11

When you desire to have a relationship with God rather than just ministry, you will seek to be in His presence. Those who are concerned with ministry will settle with a visitation from God, but those who want a permanent experience with God will seek His presence. Dwelling in the presence of the Lord should be the most essential factor in a believer's life. We cannot live without the presence of the Lord. The Bible states in Psalm 140:13, "Surely the righteous shall give thanks unto thy name: the upright shall dwell in thy presence." The presence of the Lord is so important, and yet few believers know what the presence of God really means. Many have faith that God is actually present. However, the mass only have a conviction that this is true — but conviction is not faith. The sum total of Christian living is in God's presence. The presence of the Lord is the only thing that will give us the ability to live an effective Christian life.

Chapter Nine

The Way Forward

You ask, "What is our policy?" I will say: It is to wage war, by sea, land, and air, with all our might and all the strength that God can give us ... You ask, "What is our aim?" I can answer in one word.

Victory ... at all costs. Victory in spite of all terror. Victory however long and hard the road may be; for without victory there is no survival ... We shall go on to the end. We shall fight in France. We shall fight on the seas and oceans. We shall fight with growing confidence and growing strength in the air. We shall defend our island, whatever the cost may be. We shall fight on the beaches. We shall fight on the landing grounds. We shall fight in the fields and in the streets. We shall fight in the hills. We shall never surrender.

What wonderful words to adapt to any fight against evil!

There are many declarations and speeches throughout time that have resounded and have maintained their impact and value. One of these is the words of Prime Minister Winston Churchill. Perhaps more than any other leader in the twentieth century, Winston Churchill rallied a nation to believe in what it could do. His speeches during World War II expressed firm conviction, righteous defiance, and resolution.

There is something that can certainly be learned from Winston Churchill's declaration.

His tenacity and righteous stance are noteworthy for us today. This prime minister's declaration changed the outcome of World War II. There is something powerful about a declaration that is rooted in confidence and resolution. We must take a similar stand when engaging against the enemy. Our speech must not change, and we have to speak life and not death. Proverbs 18:21 captures it in this fashion, "Death and life are in the power of the tongue: and they that love it shall eat the fruit thereof."

We must not back down, give in, or surrender. It must be forward still. The hymnal writer Henry J. Zelley (1896) perfectly captures it this way:

> Then forward still—'tis Jehovah's will, though the
> billows dash and spray. With a conq'ring tread we
> will push ahead; He'll roll the sea way.

Zelley must have had a definite understanding of God and His Word and as such recognized that the only way to grow in God was to move with God—forward still. Even if all hell is breaking loose, we must have a "forward still" mentality.

As we move forward, we must earnestly pray that God divinely positions people who are filled with His presence. We must pray for men and women who are not looking for self-gratification or glorification rather are devoted to the call and purpose of God, which is serving His people in the spirit of meekness. Many are seeking to find examples within the church that will inspire them to spiritual development and growth.

We cannot be complacent or comfortable with church as usual. We must go forward. Digression or stagnation will eventually lead to decline and self-destruction. The apostle Paul declares in Philippians 3:14: "I press toward the mark for the prize of the high calling of God in Christ Jesus."

We must never be locked in past successes or failures or believe that what we are doing or experiencing presently is the sum total of our faith. Second Peter 3:8 expresses it this way, "Be not ignorant of the devices ..."

The children of God have been silenced and made to feel unwelcomed and unwanted by so many. We cannot let the world shut us up, shut us down, shut us out, or shut us in.

The gospel writer Matthew emphatically declared, "From the days of John the Baptist until now the kingdom of heaven suffereth violence and the violent take it by force" (Matthew 11:12). The word *violent* here is referring the believer. We have to take it with focus. Passivity or a nonchalant attitude will not garner one a victorious outcome against the enemy. It requires what some may term "brute force"! In this spiritual season it requires force.

Looking Beyond (Rising from) the Ashes

Recently I kept on hearing the statement, "The phoenix rising from the ashes." In my pursuit to understand this, I discovered that the phoenix is a mythical bird that had fiery plumage and lived up to a hundred years. But at the conclusion of the phoenix's life, it settled in to its nest of twigs, which then burned ferociously, thus reducing the bird and nest to ashes. But from these ashes, a fledgling phoenix rose. This simple story is meaningful in that it speaks to the fact that despite the natural process of death, there will be the breaking forth of new life in conditions that seem abject.

History has shown the divine and diverse way in which God will deal with His people. Specifically, in every generation God always has a vessel who will proclaim His message and counsel. Time has reinforced that God will not leave Himself without a witness! In the Scriptures, God is frequently shown as looking for a man—not just any type, but a specific man. Generally God is not in pursuit of a collective but a specific person. The Scriptures clearly highlight that when God discovers a man who is willing to adhere to His requirements, he is a powerful instrument within the earth. The methods of God are oftentimes viewed as contrary to the popular thoughts of the day and as such are discounted and refuted.

In Jeremiah 5:1, God instructed Jeremiah to go through the streets of Jerusalem and find a specific man, and then He would pardon Israel. God is searching for someone that is willing to obey His commandments so that His purpose and plan can be revealed. The challenge for many of us is that we are either insensitive or too sensitive to the call of God, which can lead to dire consequences. Jonah, for example, was commissioned to go down to Nineveh, and his reluctance led him in the opposite direction, ultimately landing him in the belly of a whale. When God wants to get somebody's attention, He will at certain points cause a crisis to arise so we will stop and consider our position. God wants our attention, and if we do not pause to listen, God will sovereignly select a crisis, be it sickness or loss of employment, so we will stop and inquire of Him.

Unfortunately, some have interpreted these crises negatively and have missed God's summoning through it. Sometimes we have forgotten the fact that God is like a perfect gentleman who stands at the door and knocks (Revelation 3:20). God will not break in or intrude. He waits patiently and leaves us with the decision to open up to Him. Once we acknowledge He is

at the door and open it, it will set the stage for God to say and
do the extraordinary.

At no point do we want to force God to get our attention in a
manner that we would deem uncomfortable. Therefore, it is
incumbent for us that we submit to His will and way—even
when it feels uncomfortable. A matter of fact, most times when
God calls you, it is not necessarily something you would have
chosen to do. Jonah and Gideon are prime examples of this
and as such responded either by fleeing or hiding from God.
But God will find you anywhere you are. The Psalmist lists it
this way:

> If I ascend up into heaven, thou art there: if I make
> My bed in hell, behold thou are there: If I take the
> wings of the morning, and dwell in the uttermost
> parts of the sea.
>
> —Psalms 139:8-9

In essence, the Psalmist's hyperbolical expression clarifies
that there is absolutely no place we can go where God cannot
find us.

Stay Connected!

In the twenty-first century, technology and even globalization have spawned the constant need to be connected via the
various social mediums. Countless millions have adapted
this technological paradigm to their lifestyle to the extent that
many cannot live normally without remaining connected or
online, so to speak. Sadly, we as believers have not embraced
that same concept as it relates to God. We prefer to stay connected and updated about insignificant and even trite things
via these social mediums. But to get connected with God to

gain significant life-benefitting truths, we have willingly disregarded it as irrelevant or pointless.

If we are to move with God, we must stay connected. Yes, we have been selected to be His servants, but it is not enough just to have the label. It requires proper maintenance. There are various hindrances that may have affected our ability to regularly perform maintenance checks. Matthew 13:22 pinpoints it in this fashion:

> He also that received seed among the thorns is he that heareth the word; and the care of this world, and the deceitfulness of riches, choke the word, and he becometh unfruitful.

The gospel writer is expounding to us in this parable that this particular person did not take time or attention. As such, he or she became susceptible to the cares of the world, thus choking out the word. Once the word is choked out, the result is disconnection. Evidently, there is a true sense of disconnection between us and God. Some people don't want us to look back, but we used to see a connection, a power coming from every quarter. We beheld the glory. We have not seen that power, passion, or desire, and so there is a disconnection. We can't preach blessings every day and prosperity, even though I believe in that. You see, we have to get back to the power, faith in God, and righteousness.

God will strike at an instant when He wants to get your attention. For example, look at Saul's conversion in the book of Acts. He was on his way to persecute the church, but God demonstrated His might and changed him. God will find you wherever you are. You might think you are ordinary or even consider yourself a nobody, or you might have been told that you are gifted. But somehow you have felt that the commentary of others is unfitting or untrue and have felt comfortable with mediocrity. The life of Gideon shows us one who felt insignificant and went and hid. How many times have we fallen into that trap and as result resorted to flight … and are hiding! Why do we hide? What are the reasons for such actions?

The sad reality is that many believe that they are connected to God because they are members of a church. Unfortunately, being a member of church family does not guarantee connection to the Lord. Misconceptions of this sort cripple the minds of many believers. Some are battling with the uncertainty of who they are in God and whether God has called them. To bring it further, some wonder whether God has discounted them in light of their shortcomings and sins. These convoluted perspectives have impaired so many that they cannot make strides forward in the system of God.

There are mighty men and women who are wondering whether they have value in the Kingdom of God. You may be pondering why no one has noticed or even acknowledged what the Lord has equipped you to do. It must be underscored that nobody may ever tell or confirm your role and function in your church, but God operates on a different set of rules or paradigm. God chooses the base, undesirable, and unrecognized person for His glory.

Many times we can be fooled into believing that God will always use the persons of repute. God always goes against the grain. He will get the older to serve the younger and the last will become first. God never conforms to the ideals, expectations, and preferences of men. He operates sovereignly and righteously. The season of obscurity is a vital part of the process before promotion. The process is necessary.

Many times we have tried to validate and establish ourselves in God's design. But when we come to the point of acknowledging that it is God only who gives the increase, then and only then will we come to terms that our efforts to make it are futile. When one's season comes, it does not matter how long, hard, or dark the process was—it is your time. When the season of promotion happens, there is no human or supernatural power that can restrict you from receiving all that God has for you. But it is vital that there is understanding to one's season. Otherwise it could be mistaken or missed. Also, when it is one's season, it is not predicated on one's abilities, works, or personal strengths or resolve. It is a divine choice made by God.

Contrary to what we have been ingrained to believe, God uses the flawed and even the insignificant. The Bible presents the lives of men and women that were not perfect in any way. But their willingness to conform to His divine plan and purpose exemplified the greatness of who they were called to be. For example, in Deuteronomy 34:10, the Bible verifies that there has not arisen another man like His servant Moses. This account goes further to state that Moses was the only man who spoke to God face to face, and God talked to him mouth to mouth. But beneath this divine encounter with God Himself was a man who was flawed and prohibited from entering into the Promised Land because he failed to sanctify the people before God (Deuteronomy 32:48–52).This flaw only reminds us that God does not look for or choose the perfect. But rather, the imperfect becomes the vessel God can fashion and tailor to perfection.

The Psalmist David is another outstanding example of how God can use a flawed individual. There is no record in Scripture of another person who had a penitent heart before the Lord like David. David's love for God transcended above all of the natural possessions and applause of men. As a matter of fact, the book of Psalms reveals the heartbeat of David. Praise and jubilation to God were the resounding echo of this musician throughout this chorus book—the Psalms. He undergirds the central responsibility of man and states, "Oh, that men would praise the Lord for his goodness, and for his wonderful works to the children of men!" (Psalm 197:15).

David clearly understood the purpose of man and responded like no other in Scripture. This psalmist, musician, prophet, and king did not allow his status, clout, and worldly possessions to bridle his expression before the Lord. It was only to worship the Almighty that mattered. When we come back to the realization that everything else is secondary and that true worship before the Lord is to be of foremost importance, then and only then will we be positioned to move forward.

The Bible goes further to express that David was a man after God's own heart. David alone in Scripture became a reference point to follow. What a commendation to be classified as a man after God's own heart. Beyond the blatant sins of David, the God-fearing heart of David superseded his sins. Isn't it something that God does not evaluate or assess us on what we've done? Rather, He deals with who we are. Put differently, God uses a spiritual exchange system that simply cannot be understood rationally, because it cannot be rationalized. David came to this revelation and declared that if God were to count our sins, no one could stand (Psalm 130:3).

David understood that sin will separate one from God. His personal failures became the catalyst to emphasizing the nature of God. David received direct responses from God as to what He required. In hearing the verdict of God, David changed his spiritual posture to repentance. In acknowledgment of his sins, David sorrowfully declared, "Against thee, thee only, have I sinned, and done this evil in thy sight: that thou mightest be justified when thou speakest, and be clear when thou judgest" (Psalm 51:4).

David, being convinced of his sin, poured out his soul to God in prayer for mercy and grace. This act of David is the indicator of how to move with God. If we have missed the mark or fallen into the trap of the devil, true repentance is the right way back to God. Uniquely, the Greek words that are translated *repent* and *repentance* are defined as "to carry a sense of reversal or to change direction" (www.bibestudytools.com.2010). In other words, repentance will change one's direction and will poise one to stride forward.

When the believer has come to the understanding of his or her status in Christ, he or she can engage in spiritual combat. When there is acceptance to what God has called us, it will empower us in the fight. The Bible pointedly identifies, "Ye are a chosen generation, a royal priesthood, an holy nation, a peculiar people; that ye should shew forth the praises of him who hath called you out of darkness into his marvellous light" (1 Peter 2:9).

The New Testament writers specifically reiterated to believers of their call or position in Christ. The writers knew that if believers accepted God's classification of who they were, they would be able to wage war from the vantage point of authority and victory. Romans 8:37 puts it this way: "Nay, in all these things we are more than conquerors through him that loved us."

Paul the apostle had the revelation that our position in Christ is greater than what we oftentimes perceive or understand. But we are more than conquerors. Therefore, we can no longer disregard our God-given authority and seek alternative methods for our problems. That is why Paul in his writings exhorts the church to be watchful of unseen warfare and of the need for the believer to dress for the warfare. Second Corinthians 10:4–5 declares, "For the weapons of our warfare are not carnal, but mighty through God in the pulling down of strongholds; casting down imaginations, and every high thing that exalteth itself against the knowledge of God, and bringing into captivity every thought to the obedience of Christ." Sadly, many do not realize that spiritual warfare is not an option or a choice. We will all have to engage in combat! The only choice we have is whether we will be equipped and ready to fight or whether we will be casualties.

This is the time for the believer to be dressed for the fight. Ephesians 6:11 instructs, "Put on the whole armour of God, that ye may be able to stand against the wiles of the devil."

It is very important to highlight that the garments for warfare are not provided or prepared by man. Rather it is God who provides the armour that is necessary to obtain victory. It is through adherence that the believer is poised for combat against the powers of darkness. Yes, the experience of warfare can be wearying and daunting, but Paul tells us, "Finally, my brethren, be strong in the Lord, and in the power of his might."

The apostle knew that the believer would have to contend with great and mighty foes, and in order to meet them, the believer had to be clothed in the panoply of the Christian soldier. It goes further to exhort that the believer put on all the strength that will enable the believer to confront and contend with the enemy. In the commencement of Paul's exhortation, he reminds the Ephesian brethren that it is only by the strength of the Lord that victory could be gained.

Ziklag—Recovery Is Coming!

In 1 Samuel 29–30 and 2 Samuel 1, the reader witnesses the triumphs, defeats, and woes of the anointed minstrel, David.

The anointing of David set in motion the many challenges and tests he endured. When one is anointed, one will experience the backlash of the devil. It is an inevitable experience of the anointed vessel the Lord uses. This account records that when David and his men returned back to Ziklag, they discovered that the Amalekites had invaded their habitation. The Amalekites attacked and burned Ziklag and took the wives of David and his men as captives.

When David and his men saw that their town was burned and that their wives were taken, they cried until they could cry no more. There will be times in the Christian journey when the challenges that the believer will encounter may cause him or her to cry. But weeping is vital, as it comes before joy that comes in the morning. The backdrop of this calamity left David greatly troubled because the people considered stoning him. But in the immediacy of this chaotic and stressful moment, David encouraged himself. This action of David is an example for us. First, David did not allow this situation to distract him from gaining strength in the moment of abject despair. David encouraged himself. When trouble comes, it depletes one's strength and spiritual wit and sensibility. But trouble is a vehicle that God uses to show forth His might and power to us.

David's perspective changed. When there is a change in perspective, there will be a change in the response to trouble. But even in the face of being stoned by his comrades, David ran to the Lord. Therefore, when we are in trouble, we should run to the Lord, which is the only way toward clarity and victory. What is unique in this case is that David did not place blame on someone else, retaliate, or even attempt to run away but rather tried to get "connected" to the Lord.

David requested that Abiathar the priest bring him the ephod. In other words, David needed to redress. When we are in trouble, we have to redress and put on the garment of praise or prayer to get the divine perspective. It must be pointed out here that the ephod was the garment that the priest wore to assist in his petition for guidance from the Lord. The Bible states that Abiathar brought David the ephod, and David inquired of the Lord whether he should pursue the Amalekites. God responded that he should pursue. The outcome was that David recovered all!

This account gives strategies that will make us victors in our trials. First, your perspective of how you view and deal with trouble must change. Otherwise trouble will keep you confined in horror of the details. But when a God perspective is shed on your trouble, it will not seem or feel insurmountable or life-damaging. Rather, hope and assurance will begin to arise in the midst of the tension and chaos. Second, get connected to God. Once you get God involved in the matter, there must be a divine shift in the outcome—recovery and restoration.

These odd responses of David in calamity are tools we can use to move with God even in the hard times. We must readjust our spiritual outlook to receive from God. God is area specific and wants us to follow Him. When we follow Him, He will lead us to greater heights. But if we continue to follow humanistic thought or ideals, we will never walk into deeper places. It is time to decide—am I in the pathway that ushers me into the infinite wonders of God, or am I in a maze of pseudo-Christianity? Arguably, we have allowed the pursuit of ministry and power, discord, church politics, and thwarted perspectives of God to have us wandering around in the wilderness. Yes, we have been freed from the bondage of the world—but wandering around in the wilderness, eating manna, and experiencing the cloud cover by day and the pillar of fire by night are not the zenith of God's plan. God's desire is that we would move with Him. Encounter Him on the lofty tops of the mount and in the valley, walk through the parted Jordan, and step out of the boat and on to the instability of water. It is time to move forward. There is a sign to look at — the cross. Follow the Way, the Truth, and the Life — Jesus Himself. It is the only way!

Our biblical principles express that confusion, disunity, egotism, and rebellion to name a few are not indicators that point to Christ. Rather, it suggests that there is infection that eventually leads to spiritual dysfunction or paralyses. Living with or believing that such traits are something that we can continue to "sweep under the carpet" or consciously shrug off is no longer acceptable. If change is what is sincerely desired, then there will come a point that we must come to terms with our spiritual condition and decide, "I will not stay and die in this position." Like the lepers in 2 Kings 7:3 who were at the entrance of the gate and said one to another, "Why sit we here until we die?"

Leprosy, as we know, is a devastating disease that attacks the appearance of man; it damages or disfigures the limbs, nerves, and tissue of the body and can infect others. As in the natural so in the supernatural — spiritual leprosy can have serious impact on the body of Christ. In other words, the leprosy of disunity, confusion, and rebellion can no longer remain untreated as explored in the earlier chapters. This is the season for us to get up from this infected state and move to place of spiritual wholeness, nourishment, and wealth. We can no longer live in the realm of spiritual depravity and believe it is a tolerable status. It is high time that we choose to move forward with God! We cannot procrastinate or accept mediocrity as the norm. This is the time that we speak to ourselves and embrace spiritual fulfillment and development in the presence of the Lord! Move forward!

References

Barber, Wayne. *That we might know His Power.* Accessed December 20, 2011. http://www.preceptaustin.org/ephesians_118-20_by_wayne_barber.htm

Conner, Mark. *Unique Church Building.* Accessed December 20, 2011. http://markconner.typepad.com/catch_the_wind/2009/04/unique-church-buildings.html

Conner, Mark. *Transforming Your Church.* Accessed December 22, 2011. http://markconner.typepad.com/catch_the_wind/files/transforming_your_church_summary.doc

Damazio, Frank. *The Gate church: Realizing the Authority, Power, and results God wants for your church.* Portland, OR: City Christian Publishing, 2000.

"Faith." *Bible Knowledge.* Accessed July 3, 2011. http://www.bible-knowledge.com.

"Focus." *The Free Dictionary.* Accessed April 7, 2011. http://www.Thefreedictionary.com.

Honor Books. *God's Little Lessons for Leaders.* Tulsa, OK: Honor Books, 2001.

Lamm, Norman. *Faith and Doubt: Studies in Traditional Jewish Thoughts.* Jersey City, NJ: KTAV Publishing House, 2006.

"Loggerheads." *Hyper Dictionary.* Accessed November 2011. http://www.hyperdictionary.com.

Mitchell, Antonio L. "Biblical Meaning of Numbers—Biblical Numerology." *Christian Resources Today (2008–2011).* Accessed July 3, 2011.

http://www.christian-resources-today.com/biblical-meaning-of-numbers.html.

Mouton, Harold K. *The Analytical Greek Lexicon Revised.* Grand Rapids, MI: Zondervan Publishing House, 1978.

"Stagnation." *The Free Dictionary.* Accessed April 2011. http://www.thefreedictionary.com.

Sanders, Oswald J. *Spiritual Leadership.* Chicago: Moody Press, 1980, 20.

Sheets, Dutch. *Authority in Prayer: Praying with Power and Purpose.* Grand Rapids, MI: Bethany House Publishers, 2006.

Strong, James. "Deilias." *The Exhaustive Concordance of the Bible.* Ontario: Woodside Bible Fellowship, 1995.

"Theocracy." *Christ Notes Bible Dictionary.* Accessed July 3, 2011. http://www.christnotes.org/dictionary.php?dict=ebd&id=3633.

Penfold, Michael. J. "The Purpose Driven Church (a Critique)." Accessed July 3, 2011. http://www.webtruth.org/articles/church-issues-30/the-purpose-driven-church-(a-critique)-59.html.

The King James Version Amplified Bible Parallel Edition. Grand Rapids, MI: Zondervan Corporation, 1995.

The Holy Bible: King James Version. Electronic edition of the 1769 edition of the 1611 Authorized Version. Oak Harbor, WA: Logos Research Systems, Inc., 1995.

The Promise Contemporary English Version Holy Bible. Nashville: Thomas Nelson Publishers, 1997.

Vine, W. E. *Vine's Expository Dictionary of Old and New Testament Words.* Edited by F. F. Bruce. Old Tappan, NJ: F. H. Revell Co., 1981.

Williams, E. E. *The Best of All.* Indianapolis, Indiana: Christ Temple., 1898, 104.

Webster's New International Dictionary (Unabridged), 2nd ed., Springfield, MA: G & C Merriam Company, 1961.

"Just going to church" famous Christian quotes, December 14. http://www.goodreads.com/quotes/show/27312